The Enduring Color Line in U.S. Athletics

Sports are an integral part of American society. Millions of dollars are spent every year on professional, collegiate, and youth athletics, and participation in and viewing of these sports both alter and reflect how one perceives the world. Beamon and Messer deftly explore sports as a social construction, and more significantly, the large role race and ethnicity play in sports and consequently sports' influence on modern race relations. This text is ideal for courses on Sport and Society as well as Race and Ethnicity.

Krystal Beamon is an Assistant Professor of Sociology and Faculty Associate in the Center of African American Studies at the University of Texas at Arlington. She received her bachelor's, master's, and PhD from Oklahoma State University, where she was an All-American Track and Field athlete. Her research interests are race and ethnicity, the sociology of sport, and the contemporary African-American experience. Recent publications, found in the *Journal of Black Studies* and the *Journal of African-American Studies*, explore the intersection of race and sport while examining the experience of African-American male elite athletes.

Chris M. Messer is an Associate Professor of Sociology at Colorado State University–Pueblo. His research interests include social movements, organizational deviance, and criminology. His research has focused on riots and organizational/community response. He has also examined similar responses to environmental contamination in rural settings. Some of his articles have been published in outlets including *The Sociological Quarterly*, *Deviant Behavior*, *Sociological Spectrum*, *Journal of Social History*, and *Journal of Black Studies*.

 University Readers™
Reading Materials Evolved.

THE SOCIAL ISSUES
COLLECTION™

 Routledge
Taylor & Francis Group

Framing 21st Century Social Issues

The goal of this new, unique Series is to offer readable, teachable "thinking frames" on today's social problems and social issues by leading scholars. These are available for view on http://routledge.customgateway.com/routledge-social-issues.html.

For instructors teaching a wide range of courses in the social sciences, the Routledge *Social Issues Collection* now offers the best of both worlds: originally written short texts that provide "overviews" to important social issues *as well as* teachable excerpts from larger works previously published by Routledge and other presses.

As an instructor, click to the website to view the library and decide how to build your custom anthology and which thinking frames to assign. Students can choose to receive the assigned materials in print and/or electronic formats at an affordable price.

Available

Body Problems
Running and Living Long in a Fast-Food Society
Ben Agger

Sex, Drugs, and Death
Addressing Youth Problems in American Society
Tammy Anderson

The Stupidity Epidemic
Worrying About Students, Schools, and America's Future
Joel Best

Empire Versus Democracy
The Triumph of Corporate and Military Power
Carl Boggs

Contentious Identities
Ethnic, Religious, and Nationalist Conflicts in Today's World
Daniel Chirot

The Future of Higher Education
Dan Clawson and Max Page

Waste and Consumption
Capitalism, the Environment, and the Life of Things
Simonetta Falasca-Zamponi

Rapid Climate Change
Causes, Consequences, and Solutions
Scott G. McNall

The Problem of Emotions in Societies
Jonathan H. Turner

Outsourcing the Womb
Race, Class, and Gestational Surrogacy in a Global Market
France Winddance Twine

Changing Times for Black Professionals
Adia Harvey Wingfield

The Enduring Color Line in U.S. Athletics

Krystal Beamon

University of Texas, Arlington

Chris M. Messer

Colorado State University–Pueblo

Routledge
Taylor & Francis Group

NEW YORK AND LONDON

First published 2014
by Routledge
711 Third Avenue, New York, NY 10017

Simultaneously published in the UK
by Routledge
2 Park Square, Milton Park, Abingdon, Oxon OX14 4RN

Routledge is an imprint of the Taylor & Francis Group, an informa business

Library of Congress Cataloging in Publication Data
The enduring color line in U.S. athletics / Krystal Beamon, Chris M. Messer.
   pages cm. — (Framing 21st century social issues)
   Includes bibliographical references and index.
   Racism in sports—United States. 2. Sports team mascots—Social aspects—
United States. I. Messer, Chris M. II. Title.
   GV706.32.B43 2014
   796.089—dc23
   2013023153

ISBN: 978-0-415-62671-2 (pbk)
ISBN: 978-1-315-87961-1 (ebk)

Typeset in Garamond and Gill Sans
by EvS Communication Networx, Inc.

University Readers (www.universityreaders.com): Since 1992, University
Readers has been a leading custom publishing service, providing reasonably priced,
copyright-cleared, course packs, custom textbooks, and custom publishing services
in print and digital formats to thousands of professors nationwide. The Routledge
Custom Gateway provides easy access to thousands of readings from hundreds of
books and articles via an online library. The partnership of University Readers and
Routledge brings custom publishing expertise and deep academic content together
to help professors create perfect course materials that are affordable for students.

Printed and bound in the United States of America by Publishers Graphics,
LLC on sustainably sourced paper.

Contents

Series Foreword

The early years of the 21st century have been a time of paradoxes. Growing prosperity and the growth of the middle classes in countries such as Brazil, China, India, Russia and South Africa have been accompanied by climate change, environmental degradation, labor exploitation, gender inequalities, state censorship of social media, governmental corruption, and human rights abuses. Sociologists offer theories, concepts, and analytical frames that enable us to better understand the challenges and cultural transformations of the 21st century. How can we generate new forms of collective knowledge that can help solve some of our local, global, and transnational problems?

We live in a world in which new communication technologies and products such as cell phones, iPads, and new social media such as Facebook, Google, and Skype have transformed online education, global communication networks, local and transnational economies, facilitated revolutions such as the "Arab Spring," and generated new forms of entertainment, employment, protest, and pleasure. These social media have been utilized by social justice activists, political dissidents, educators, entrepreneurs, and multinational corporations. They have also been a source of corporate deviance and government corruption used as a form of surveillance that threatens democracy, privacy, creative expression, and political freedoms.

The goal of this series is to provide accessible and innovative analytical frames that examine a wide range of social issues including social media whose impact is local, global, and transnational. Sociologists are ideally poised to contribute to a global conversation about a range of issues such as the impact of mass incarceration on local economies, medical technologies, health disparities, violence, torture, transnational migration, militarism, and the AIDS epidemic.

The books in this series introduce a wide range of analytical frames that dissect and discuss social problems and social pleasures. These books also engage and intervene directly with current debates within the social sciences over how best to define, rethink, and respond to the social issues that characterize the early 21st century. The contributors to this series bring together the works of classical sociology into dialogue with contemporary social theorists from diverse theoretical traditions including but not limited to feminist, Marxist, and European social theory.

Readers do not need an extensive background in academic sociology to benefit from these books. Each book is student-friendly in that we provide glossaries of terms for the uninitiated that appear in bold in the text. Each chapter ends with questions for further thought and discussion. The books are the ideal level for undergraduates because they are accessible without sacrificing a theoretically sophisticated and innovative analysis.

This is the fourth year of our Routledge Social Issues Book series. Ben Agger was the former editor of this series during its first three years. These books explore contemporary social problems in ways that introduce basic sociological concepts in the social sciences, cover key literature in the field, and offer original diagnoses. Our series includes books on a broad range of topics including climate change, consumption, eugenics, torture, surrogacy, gun violence, the Internet, and youth culture.

Krystal Beamon and Chris Messer provide a rare comparative analysis of the experiences of three ethnic groups in US sports: Blacks, Native Americans, and Hispanics (Latinos). The sports industry has structured the lives of some of the most visible role models in Black and Hispanic communities and has had a paradoxical impact on the lives of women and men who become professional athletes. Excelling in sports, rather than academia, is perceived by many as a route for social mobility. Yet we learn from the authors of this book that sport is also a "contested terrain," where racial and ethnic stereotypes and inequalities are reproduced. This book will inspire the reader to think more critically about the social costs of professional sports as an idealized career choice among the most economically oppressed racial and ethnic minorities in the United States. In a capitalist economy in which increasing numbers of the poor are denied a good education professional sport remains an arena of economic refuge. However, the hypervisibility and idealization of star athletes sends messages to youth that may prevent them from considering other avenues of achievement. This book is ideal for courses on social inequality, race and ethnic relations, cultural studies, sociology of sports, and American studies.

France Winddance Twine
Series Editor

Preface

A cool fall morning, black and gold everything, everywhere. I am running and screaming down the field as my kindergartener scores his second touchdown of the day. I feel the familiar sense of pride that outstanding athletic performances can give. My son is the size of an eight-year-old and outweighs the others by at least 10 pounds, but he can run fast enough to make it down the field untouched. People are already discussing his future NFL career with me—even though he is only five years old. As a mom I am proud; as a sociologist I am cautious and protective, not wanting him to begin to develop an identity around his athletic talents. Half-time rolls around and we are up by two touchdowns in a flag football game for preschoolers and kindergarteners that does not officially keep score. Yet the parents and everyone in the league know that our team is undefeated. Equipped with my black-and-gold "Football Mom" T-shirt, I prepare to escort my son across the field for our half-time Homecoming festivities. I look around and realize the importance of this ritual. Collectively, the amount of money, time, energy, and shared emotion invested on this field makes this peewee football league the primary focus for many of the families in our large suburban neighborhood.

I am no stranger to this way of life. Throughout my own childhood, my household was structured around sports. My brothers played football, basketball, and baseball. I was a gymnast and track and field star. For as long as I can remember, Saturdays meant baseball diamonds, football fields, track and field stadiums, basketball courts, and long hours practicing back handsprings and double twisting layouts. It was simply life as usual for my family and most of the families that I knew. I had an anonymous sponsor paying for my track and field travel and equipment by the time I was 10, and my brother had professional baseball scouts at his games as a pre-teen. My oldest brother went on to play Division I basketball in college on a full scholarship, my middle brother played over a decade in the Major League Baseball system, and I ran track on a full scholarship earning a Division I collegiate All-American honor. Sports have been the biggest part of my life for most of my life, and have shaped my career as a sociologist and researcher. As a sociologist, former elite athlete, and sister to a 30-something retired professional athlete, I began to see sports in a different light.

I began to uncover systematically the social significance of sport in America and its connection to race and race relations. Sports, as a **social construction**, influence how people feel, think, and live their lives while reflecting and creating important aspects of culture, shared experiences, and shared identities (Coakley 2010).

Sports make up an important **social institution** in American society that holds a prominent position as a component of our culture. It is one of the great pillars of American industry as a profitable form of entertainment closely connected to the economy, education, family, and many other spheres of social life in America. Accordingly, this important American institution has generated several areas of interest in the study of society and human behavior. Sociologists and other scholars have noted the many fascinating phenomena that exist in youth, collegiate, and professional athletics. Sports mirror the human experience (Eitzen 2012): the triumphs, the trials, the excitement, the defeat, the victories, and the drive to win and overcome adversity. They are a microcosm of society and reflect both the great successes and ills of American life. In this book, my co-author and I examine the relationship between race and sport in America; how sport has both reflected and influenced modern race relations. We will emphasize the intersection of race and sport and dissect the ever-prominent racial components of youth, collegiate, and elite athletics.

Krystal Beamon

Acknowledgments

I (Beamon) would like to thank my colleague Beth Anne Shelton for her invaluable support. Your early readings and suggestions assisted tremendously. I would also like to acknowledge Ben Agger for his guidance throughout the publication process.

We would like to acknowledge our mentor Dr. Patricia Bell for all of her encouragement, assistance, and for shaping us both into the sociologists that we have become. Finally, we would especially like to thank our editor, France Winddance Twine. Your guidance throughout this process has strengthened our work and we're deeply appreciative for all you've done.

1:   The Color Line in Athletics

On February 3, 2012, a previously unknown basketball player for the New York Knicks became an overnight sensation. Jeremy Lin, a Harvard graduate, had been previously waived by two teams and secured a spot on the Knicks after injuries depleted the team's point guard position. Lin was inserted into the game and immediately captured America's attention as he made an unexpected and dramatic impact, scoring 25 points. Three nights later he made his first career start and scored 28 points. His success continued throughout the remainder of the season against some of the NBA's greatest stars and a period known as "Linsanity" was underway. However, public fixation wasn't merely centered on Lin and his immediate success: it was also connected to Lin's Asian American **race** and **ethnicity**, which is a rarity in professional U.S. sports (Pandya 2012). In fact, Asians make up only 1 percent of all **National Basketball Association (NBA)** players (Lapchick 2011). The relationship between sports and race is deep and reflects various dimensions of U.S. society that stretch far beyond athletic participation. As we will show, access to sport, commonly held stereotypes about athletes, and social change in sport are all intertwined with the issues of race and its inseparable connection to gender and social class. Also, patterns that exist in sport (access, images of athletes, and social change) mirror larger patterns in U.S. society in a quite fascinating way.

The sports industry in the United States is a product of American values that reward individualism, materialism, and consumption. Americans spend more than $25 billion a year on athletics (Quinn 2009). In a nation driven by **capitalism**, an economic system fueled by competition and private ownership, athletics reinforces the U.S. obsession and emphasis upon individualism and success. Capitalism shapes the way that professional sports are organized at the local, community, and professional levels. For example, youth sports have become increasingly privatized, and the average American family spends nearly $2,000 a year on sports for their children (Coffey 2010). Certain sports require the purchase of expensive equipment and private lessons in addition to the regular costs of travel and club membership and fees. As a consequence, access to sport opportunities is organized around money, thereby limiting access to opportunities and effectively segregating youth sports by race, ethnicity, and class (Farry 2008; Wells 2008). This pattern explains why Blacks, Hispanics, and Native Americans are less likely to join the professional ranks of golfers and hockey and soccer players—because these groups are disproportionately poor and the financial costs associated with training, playing, and traveling are exorbitant (Saint Onge and Krueger 2011).

Therefore, sociologists and other scholars refer to the **color line** in U.S. sports (Miller and Wiggins 2004). This term refers to the systematic legal separation, or state-sanctioned **segregation**, also known as **Jim Crow** segregation. This system sustained White supremacy after slavery was abolished, and institutionalized separate educational institutions, churches, residential neighborhoods, professional sports, and other forms of social life. This system remained in place until the late 1960s and early 1970s. It has been replaced by what is known as **de facto segregation**. Segregation fuels and perpetuates economic and social inequality. "The problem of the twentieth century," stated Du Bois, "is the problem of the color line—the relation of the darker to the lighter races of men" (Du Bois 1903: 54). Segregation privileged Whites in education, transportation, voting, phone booths, restaurants, and most other components of **social institutions** (Woodward 1966). Even though segregation has ended as a legal principle, sociologists point to continued realms of **institutional racism** (Carmicheal and Hamilton 1967; Lopez 2004; Weinberg 1996), where a color line highlights the social, political, and economic disparities that routinely privilege Whites, including in sports (Burgos 2009; Gallagher 2012; Miller and Wiggins 2004). Even gaining access to sports and success, though, doesn't thwart institutional racism. Sustained patterns of racial inequality and discrimination exist even within the most integrated sports and at the highest levels. For instance, in their study of NBA referees and the fouls called from the 1991–1992 season through the 2003–2004 year, Price and Wolfers (2010) find that officiating consists of an "own-race bias," meaning that White referees call more fouls against Black players and Black referees call more fouls against White players at statistically significant levels. A number of interpretations are offered for this pattern, but the pattern itself indicates that perceptions of race, no matter how subtle they may be, pervade even the most integrated professional sport in the United States (Lapchick 2011).

It's also important to acknowledge that sports are "gendered organizations" (Acker 1990), meaning that athletics, like all social institutions, is structured in ways that privilege men over women. At a more overt level, this can be viewed through the differences in popularity of professional leagues of play. For example, the average attendance at an NBA game is 17,273 (ESPN 2013) compared to the average attendance of 8,203 at a WNBA game (Dorish 2011a). Or consider the wage gap, where the average NBA salary is $5.15 million (Aschburner 2011) compared to the *highest* salary of a WNBA player allowed by rule, which is $101,500 (Dorish 2011b). Importantly, as a gendered organization, the WNBA is owned by the NBA and therefore its rules, policies, and procedures are largely written for women by men.

Institutional **sexism** and racism are pervasive across all sports and at all levels of play, not just in the professional ranks. For example, in 1972, **Title IX** of the Civil Rights Act was passed. The goal of this legislation, which was to eliminate gender discrimination in federally funded social institutions, led to a substantial increase in women's athletics participation and the individual and social benefits that come along

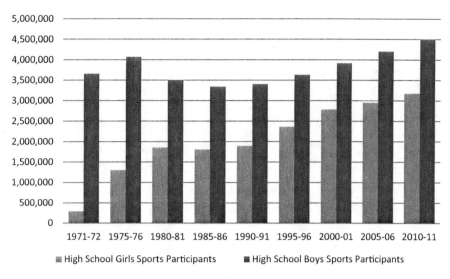

Source: National Federation of State High School Associations 2011

Figure 1.1 High School Girls' and Boys' Sports Participation 1971–2011

with sport involvement. Figure 1.1 illustrates the considerable growth in the sports participation of girls from 1972–2011 due to the implementation of Title IX. In collegiate athletics alone, the number of women student-athletes grew by 456 percent due to Title IX guidelines (National Collegiate Athletic Association 2006b).

This legislation provided social change on an institutional level, influencing the lives of millions of girls and women. By expanding the number of sports available to women at all levels of play, it would appear that the United States has increasingly provided females more opportunities to experience the same virtues of sport that were once offered primarily to men. Indeed, athletics reaffirms our belief in the **American Dream**, which is a set of beliefs that values equality of opportunity and promotes the idea that the United States is a **meritocracy**, an ideal system where rewards are distributed based solely on individual effort and achievement. However, we would not have needed the Civil Rights Act or Title IX if this had been the case.

Although Title IX has significantly increased the number of females in sport, high schools where Black teens attend are less likely to offer the same range of women's sports that yield scholarships in college (Pickett, Dawkins, and Braddock 2009). For example, from 1991 to 2000, the number of women's collegiate soccer teams increased from 318 to 811, but this sport, in addition to softball, crew, and volleyball (other "new growth sports" offered more and more with scholarships at the collegiate level), is less likely to appear in high schools located in poor communities where Blacks and Latinas are more likely to reside. According to Pickett, Dawkins, and Braddock (2009), "The effect of Title IX at the high school level may be to maintain the 'funneling' of Black female athletes into the two main sports (basketball and track and field), while White female athletes benefit the most from the addition of new sports and programs" (p. 88). This pattern illustrates that institutional racism and sexism can go hand in hand, and as we show, characterize both men's and women's sports.

Sports have long been considered a site of **hegemonic masculinity**, where men are afforded a position of domination over women and such an arrangement becomes legitimized or accepted within the larger **culture** (Connell 2005). In any system of **hegemony**, a ruling class subtly manipulates lower classes into accepting their subordinate position through the espousal of a dominant set of values and culture that disproportionately empowers and benefits the elite (Gramsci 1971). According to Gee (2009), sport is considered a prime venue for displaying masculinity and the associated cultural ideals such as "aggression, heterosexuality, muscularity, the suppression of fear, intentional physical demonstrations of **power** and dominance, and the subordinated role of women" (p. 581). As such, youth are often heard aspiring to "be like Mike," dreams that are wrapped up in nuanced images and interpretations of race and its connection to gender. This is even more pronounced among Black males as their cultural identity and masculinity are often tied to athletic participation and performance (Smith 2007; Spence 2000). But how attainable is the goal of actually becoming like Mike? Has the integration of certain sports such as basketball and football served entirely beneficial purposes for Blacks? Does the increased representation of Hispanics from various ethnic backgrounds in baseball signify that U.S. culture is increasingly embracing non-White athletes?

The Reproduction of Racial and Social Inequalities

Differential access to sport establishes a unique system of **cultural capital**, or social assets such as education, knowledge, and other advantages that provide a higher status in society. **Pierre Bourdieu** (1984) also discusses other types of capital, including economic (one's command over economic resources such as cash and investments), social (resources acquired through friendships, networks, and other interpersonal associations), and symbolic (resources acquired through honor and prestige). Those with cultural capital can convert those resources into economic and symbolic capital (Bourdieu 1984).

According to Bourdieu (1984), there are a plethora of reasons one may participate in sports, including fitness, relaxation, and establishing/maintaining interpersonal relationships. Others participate for profit. Regardless of the motivation, sport participation can produce and reproduce patterns of cultural capital. Observe a local golf course and you'll likely notice that most, if not all, of the present golfers are White. Participating in sports such as golf is a way to display one's social status, as anyone knows that frequent participation in golf is costly. Golf therefore becomes associated with a middle- to upper-middle-class lifestyle and the sport effectively blocks economically disadvantaged groups from gaining access, or at least from gaining enough access to become highly skilled (Warde 2006). Therefore, it's understandable that impoverished groups would be more likely to turn to sports such as basketball and football where the start-up costs of participation are less.

Is sport an equalizer and sign of racial progress? Or are professional sports another avenue that can subtly perpetuate and reproduce racial and ethnic **stereotypes** and maintain social inequality? This book addresses these questions. According to Douglas Hartmann (2000), one popular view is that sports are a way out of the "ghetto"; that impoverished Blacks, in particular, can use sports to move up the economic ladder and achieve success. The biographies of professional athletes who grew up in poverty, and were able to escape this condition through their participation in sports, are abundant.

Michael Oher, whose life story inspired the blockbuster movie *The Blind Side* (dir. Hancock 2009), grew up in foster care and homeless (Oher 2011). Oher signed a $13.8 million contract with the Baltimore Ravens in 2009 and continues to have success in the **National Football League (NFL)** (Oher 2011). With his mother only 16, Lebron James spent his early life in foster care. Through his great athletic ability he is now a household name earning tens of millions of dollars each year playing in the NBA and signing lucrative endorsement deals with major corporations (Jones 2005). These are just two of the highly publicized rags-to-riches athlete stories that feature prominently in media portrayals.

A critique of this perspective is that sport actually serves to reproduce racial inequality and this can be seen in the similar obstacles that certain racial and ethnic groups, including Blacks and Hispanics, experience in mainstream society, such as limited career advancement potential, limited access to ownership and management positions, and fewer rewards for equal effort (Hartmann 2000). Moreover, a critique of the popular view of sport points to the fact that for every "rags-to-riches" story, there are millions of athletes that don't make it to elite levels of sport participation despite an investment of tremendous resources and effort by individuals, families, and communities.

Sociological research on the relationship between race and sports in the post-Civil Rights United States has focused primarily on White/Black segregation and integration, leaving out the important role that other racial and ethnic groups have played in the development of professional athletics. For example, Native Americans and Hispanics played **Major League Baseball (MLB)** decades prior to Jackie Robinson's debut. Recent research has focused on the absence of Blacks in managerial positions in basketball and football, particularly given the overrepresentation of Blacks as players in those same professional leagues. Yet, very little attention has been given by scholars to the absence of Latin Americans in baseball management positions even though they are overrepresented as players in baseball.

An analysis of the unequal distribution of racial and ethnic groups across various sports will illustrate contemporary discrimination. Although Blacks comprise 12 percent of the U.S. population, they make up 78 percent of NBA players, 67 percent of NFL players, and 15 percent of all Major League Baseball players (another 25 percent

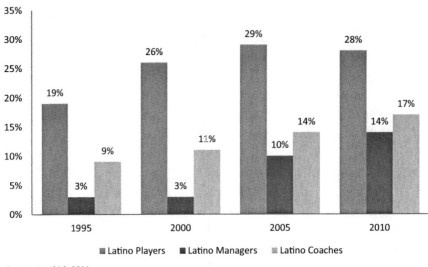

Source: Lapchick 2011

Figure 1.2 Latino Players, Managers, and Coaches in Major League Baseball 1995–2020

are Hispanic, many of Afro-Hispanic descent) (Lapchick 2011). The National Hockey League (NHL), Pro Golfers Association (PGA), and professional tennis circuit are almost exclusively White. Additionally, outside of mascots (discussed in Chapter 2), there is a noticeable underrepresentation of Native Americans (as well as Asian Americans) in most commercialized sports in America.

Patterns in race and sport reflect similar trends of institutional discrimination experienced in larger American society (Washington and Karen 2001). This is evidenced in the overrepresentation of Blacks on the field, and the virtual absence of them in decision-making administration roles in the sports industry. Black student-athletes at **Division I** universities comprise a large proportion of athletes in football and basketball, but administration, leadership, coaching, and advising positions are still largely occupied by White males. Table 1.1 shows the percentages of Black administrators and coaches at **National Collegiate Athletic Association (NCAA)** Division I universities, excluding Historically Black Universities (HBUs), for 1995–1996 and 2009–2010 (Lapchick 2011).

As illustrated in Table 1.1, Blacks have not benefited from the same opportunities in off-the-field athletics as Whites have. The same pattern holds true for other racial and ethnic groups heavily present in other sports. The result is fewer role models for Black and Hispanic student athletes. John Thompson, former Georgetown University men's basketball coach, stated, "People are able to participate in the cotton field, but not be the foreman or boss … Several kids can play at the universities but not get a job [there]" (Ley 1998, n.p.). As illustrated in Table 1.2, there are similar patterns in both the NFL and the NBA. Black athletes are largely shut out from ownership and leadership, but overrepresented as "workers" (players).

Table 1.1 Percentages of Black Administrators and Coaches at Non-HBU Division I Universities

Position	Percent Black	
	1995–96	2009–10
Director of Athletics	2.7	3.9
Associate Director of Athletics	5.9	7.6
Assistant Director of Athletics	6.7	7.4
Academic Advisor	18	17.3
Head Coach Men's Revenue Sports (football and basketball)	8	9.4

Source: Lapchick 2011

We therefore agree with Hartmann (2000) and expand on the idea in this book that sport and race is "**contested terrain**"; that is, while sport provides opportunity for success that for a long time was unavailable to many racial and ethnic groups, sport also serves to blind us to the continued impoverished state that many of these same groups experience. The success of elite Black athletes, for example, serves to perpetuate and reinforce the status quo in our culture, or the idea that through enough hard work any individual can achieve success. In reality, the probability of a high school youth making it to the professional level of sports participation (where they're finally financially compensated) is between 0.02 and 0.1 percent for the sports of basketball (men's and women's), football, baseball, ice hockey, and soccer (NCAA 2012a)! This is problematic for disadvantaged youth seeking to use sports as a means to escape "the ghetto" because education and career planning—more realistic paths to success—often become deemphasized in the process.

Viewing sport as contested terrain also requires us to consider the many stereotypes that continue to dominate everyday discourse about minority athletes and their White

Table 1.2 Percentages of Blacks in Leadership Positions in the NBA and NFL

Position	Percent Black 2009–10	
	NBA	NFL
Players	78	67
League front office	20	8.7
Majority owners	2	0
Head coaches	27	19
General managers/Directors of player personnel	23	16
Administration	16	10
Physicians	3	5
Trainers	16	17
Radio and TV announcers	18	8

Source: Lapchick 2011

counterparts. This perspective looks, for instance, at the stereotypes that are used to frame the absence of Asians in certain sports based on bodies and dieting practices (Hylton 2010). Indeed, race is talked about in sport discourse in intriguing ways. According to Buffington and Fraley (2011), "racetalk," as they label it, is polite on the surface due to its coded nature and the attempt to avoid appearing racist. For example, the next time you are watching athletic competition, pay close attention to how athletes of different racial and ethnic groups are talked about. In their study of its presentation of race, Azzarito and Harrison (2008) discovered that media have a tendency to focus on the physical prowess of Black athletes, compared to their framing of White athletes, who are portrayed as leaders with superior mental ability. Similarly, Buffington and Fraley (2011) noticed that teenagers talk about a "natural ability" Black athletes possess compared to White athletes who have to "work harder" to develop ability. According to Carrington (2010), the making of the "Black Athlete" dates back to the boxer, Jack Johnson. This perceived "super-human" athlete, still considered a sub-human character in many ways, reinforced existing stereotypes and produced new ones. The "racial signification of sports" as defined by Carrington (2010) specifies how sports "played a central role in popularizing notions of absolute biological difference" and still today "ideologies of race saturate the fabric of modern sports" (p. 3). These stereotypes of certain groups as "natural athletes" have larger societal consequences and can result in the perception that because Whites seemingly have to "try harder," they are therefore more deserving of reward, recognition, and respect.

Preview of Chapters

Subsequent chapters focus on the intersection of race and sport and will dissect the ever-prominent and visible racial components of the sporting world. Chapter II examines Native Americans' presence in sports and the controversial issue of Native American mascots. What effect does the widespread perpetuation of myopic stereotypes have on this diverse racial and cultural category of people? This debate has existed for over 30 years and continues to garner media attention. We place this presentation in the context of "contested terrain," and discuss that while some advocates of retaining these mascots use "racetalk," claiming the practice pays homage to Native Americans, other groups—including both tribes and professional organizations such as the American Psychological Association—maintain that these mascots have a negative effect on the self-esteem and identity of Native American youth.

Chapter III discusses the significant participation of Latinos in professional baseball. Arguably, the most debated issues in the sociology of race and racism in the United States are immigration policies, illegal immigration, and the fear that some immigrants are "taking over" America. That debate has filtered into baseball as the prominence of Spanish-speaking players, particularly those native to the Dominican Republic, continues to rise. We examine how the increased representation of Latino/

Hispanic baseball players is tied to both socialization patterns and economic inequalities in the region.

Chapters IV and V cover two important dimensions of Black athletic participation. Is or has professional athletics been a golden opportunity for Black athletes? Finally, we discuss the future direction of sport and sport research in Chapter VI.

DISCUSSION QUESTIONS

1. Do you think that children as young as three years of age should have access to organized sports? Explain.
2. In your view, what role has professional sport played in facilitating economic and social integration of racial minorities into the middle classes?
3. Identify two or three favorite sports teams. Who are the owners, managers, and administrators of these teams? Do these teams have women, Blacks, or Latinos in administrative positions at collegiate and professional levels? Identify three measures that you think could be employed to increase the numbers of women and ethnic minorities in administrative positions.

II: The Native American Experience: Racism and Mascots in Professional Sports

~~~×~~~

Early European contact with Native American tribes resulted in cultural and physical **genocide.** According to the 2010 census, Native Americans make up less than 1 percent of the total population of the United States of America. This once thriving group that numbered over 10 million persons and spoke over 700 languages prior to colonization is projected to make up less than 0.5 percent of the American population by 2050 (Schaefer 2011). Today, the culture and language of many tribes are extinct, with tribal elders, anthropologists, and other scholars fighting to preserve and pass on remnants of both for future generations. Compared to other racial and ethnic groups, Native Americans have the highest rates of poverty, alcoholism, and suicide, and the lowest rate of educational attainment (Center for Native American Youth 2012).

The term Native American refers to an extremely diverse group of people. Although similarities exist, each tribe has a distinct culture with varying customs, religious and spiritual beliefs, kinship and political systems, and history. Due to the wide use of stereotypes in the media, isolation of Native Americans on reservations, and the invisible nature of mixed-raced Native Americans in urban areas, most Americans conceive of "Indians" in a very narrow manner. **Pan-Indianism,** or the growing solidarity among Native Americans, has created a tendency to focus less on tribal heritage and more on common injustices that Native Americans face as a whole. A key source of frustration relates to a set of cultural stereotypes that narrowly depict Native Americans as a remnant of history filled with savagery. More specifically, according to many pan-Indian civil rights groups, the commercialization of Native American images and the use of Native American mascots perpetuate a minimalistic understanding of their diverse experiences and cultures (Nuessel 1994; Williams 2007). It's important first to discuss the historical presence of Native Americans in sport, and later, the surfacing of mascots that depict Native American images.

Native Americans in Sports

Historically, Native American tribes have been physically active in games and athletics. Traditional Native American sports such as stickball, lacrosse, archery, running, and canoeing were often connected to spiritual, political, or economic worldviews (King 2004). They were important in training children, and the outcomes often held ritual significance. In the late 19th century, Native American boarding schools were developed with aims to "kill the Indian and save the man," taking Indian children out of their homes away from their families and indoctrinating them with European language, culture, religion, and sports (Churchill 2004: 14). While many Native Americans continued to participate in traditional games and sports, this forced **assimilation**, a form of ethnic genocide in boarding schools, produced a decline in traditional games.

Organized interscholastic sports were institutionalized by European Americans as a form of cultural control. Sports were used as a tool of domination in which Native American boys learned to see their traditional games as "inferior" and were taught that there were more "civilized" ways to compete. For example, according to Gems, football "taught Indians rules, discipline, and civilization" (1998: 146), which were considered European American virtues. The White headmasters perceived sports as an effective tool in channeling males into more acceptable European roles and behavior. As an unintended consequence, many boarding schools fielded successful athletic teams in football and baseball, taking on and winning against collegiate powerhouses such as Harvard and Syracuse between 1900 and 1932 (Haggard 2004).

The Carlisle Indian School and Haskell Institute produced exceptional athletes, such as Jim Thorpe, who is considered one of the most versatile athletes in American history. A Sac and Fox tribal member, Thorpe played professional baseball, football, and basketball and also won gold medals in the 1912 Olympics for the pentathlon and decathlon. He attended the Haskell Institute in Lawrence, Kansas as a youth (Wheeler 1979). As Gems (1998) notes, athletic participation at such schools allowed Native Americans in the early 1900s to assert their racial identity,

> by providing a collective memory of self-validation and the creation of kindred heroes as they successfully tested themselves against the beliefs of Social Darwinism and dispelled notions of white dominance ... In that sense football proved to be not only an assimilative experience, but a resistive and liberating one as well.
>
> (Gems 1998: 148)

Nonetheless, there was an obvious absence of Native American athletes reaching national success between World War II and the 1964 victory of Billy Mills at the Olympic Games (King 2004). Mills began running at the Haskell Institute in Kansas as a youth and became the second Native American to win a gold medal at the Olympics (Jim Thorpe was the first). His win in the 10,000-meter run was unexpected as he competed against a world record holder from Australia, Ron Clarke (Mills 2009). Mills often discussed why many traditional Native Americans did not participate fully in organized sports. Mills believed that engaging in a sporting program that does not acknowledge cultural heritage creates a fear among Native American athletes, a fear of going too far into White society and losing one's "Indianness" while participating in mainstream sports (Simpson 2009: 291).

In 1968, the American Indian Movement (AIM) was launched in Minneapolis, Minnesota and soon thereafter spread across the country. The movement sought to address problems affecting the Native American community such as poverty, police harassment, and treaty violations. During its initial stages, the movement was known for its pan-Indian philosophy and protests. Perhaps the most famous protest occurred in 1973 at Wounded Knee, South Dakota at the Pine Ridge Indian Reservation. Armed members of the movement occupied the area in protest at Native American poverty and U.S. government treaty violations. The event culminated in a 71-day standoff with federal law enforcement and ended only after two Native Americans were killed (Banks and Erdoes 2004). Today, AIM continues to fight against the same problems of poverty and treaty violations and also actively protests the use of Native American mascots (American Indian Movement n.d.).

Other organizations such as the National Indian Athletic Association (NIAA), founded in 1973, and the Native American Sports Council (NASC), founded in1993, were created to promote athletic participation and excellence among Native American athletes throughout North America. Today, the NASC sponsors sports leagues and provides training and other forms of support to potential Olympians. These organizations support the development of Native Americans through fitness, community involvement, and boosting self-esteem (Kalambakal 2004). Formerly a colonial tool used to force Native American children of both sexes to reject their heritage and adopt European-American cultural norms, these athletic organizations employ sports to steer youngsters in a positive direction and reduce the high rates of suicide, drug and alcohol use, and gang activity on the reservations (Kalambakal 2004). Through both the NIAA and NASC, sports education, sports camps, and clinics have led to an increase in Native American participation in mainstream sports in the Olympics, college, and professional sports; however, this "trend has yet to produce the numbers experienced during the early twentieth century" (Haggard 2004: 226).

Native American athletes are hardly visible in contemporary sports. Aside from a few teams and individual athletes in segregated Indian schools, Native American sport participation has been limited by many factors. Poverty, poor health, lack of equipment and facilities, and a lack of cultural understanding by those who control sports, as well as academic unpreparedness and negative academic stereotypes of

Native American student-athletes, has limited the non-reservation sports opportunities of these athletes (Simpson 2009). This cultural group remains underrepresented as athletes at all levels despite the obvious talent and the popularity of basketball on Native American reservations. However, this talent garnered recent attention with the story of two sisters on the University of Louisville's women's basketball team, which finished as the national championship runner-up in 2013. Shone and Jude Schimmel were raised on the Umatilla Reservation in Oregon and were considered exceptional local talent. Playing a style they call "rez ball," the sisters captivated local audiences growing up. Their national success has led to an explosion of interest in basketball among the local reservation youth and a sense of pride among Native Americans in general (Block 2013).

Youth sports are associated with forms of capital including social capital that can advantage Native youth. For example, children and youth who participate in organized sports perform better academically, are less likely to drink or do drugs, have higher self-esteem, and lower rates of obesity and diabetes (Bailey 2006; Broh 2002; Eitle and Eitle 2002; Ewing et al. 2002; Pate et al. 2000). Native Americans are underrepresented in youth sport leagues and have higher rates of alcoholism, high school dropout, suicide, obesity, and diabetes than any other minority group (Bachman et al. 1991; Center for Native American Youth 2012; Gray and Smith 2003). Greater participation may be a valuable resource for Native American youth.

Native Americans also remain underrepresented at the elite levels. In NCAA Division I, II, and III sports, Native American men and women make up 0.4 percent of student-athletes (NCAA 2012b). As illustrated in Figure 2.1, White men and women make up the largest majority of NCAA Division I, II, and III student-athletes in most sports, while Native Americans are widely underrepresented in all sports. In fact, even in lacrosse, a sport thought to have roots in the Cherokee traditional game "stickball," Native American men and women make up less than 0.5 percent of collegiate players. The highest representation of Native American NCAA student-athletes is seen in softball, where Native American women make up 0.7 percent of all players.

While they are underrepresented as students on college campuses along with most minority groups, Native Americans are far less represented as collegiate athletes compared to Blacks and Hispanics. In fact, the most visible representation of Native American culture in popular commercialized sports is found among mascots. In addition to the many professional sports teams, hundreds of high schools and close to 100 universities have Native American images for mascots and nicknames—not to mention the countless little league and peewee teams that follow suit using these images to represent their teams. Along with class and access issues in youth sports, these disparaging mascots may be linked to the lack of participation of Natives in youth sports and the benefits that go along with participation.

	All sports (Division I)	Football	Basketball	Track and field	Soccer	Baseball	Softball	Lacrosse
☑ White Men	62.5	55.1	43.5	64.9	68.5	84.7		88.2
☑ White Women	70.6		55.7	66.2	80.7		81.1	88.2
☑ Black Men	29.4	35.4	45.5	21.6	7.2	3.9		2.7
☑ Black Women	16		32.7	20.4	3.7		5.8	2.8
☑ Hispanic Men	4.2	3	2.8	4.6	9.9	5.6		1.5
☑ Hispanic Women	4.2		3	4.1	5.6		6	2.1
☑ Native American Men	0.4	0.5	0.2	0.4	0.2	0.4		0.3
☑ Native American Women	0.4		0.4	0.4	0.3		0.7	0.2
☑ Asian Men	2	0.7	0.5	1.4	1.6	0.9		0.9
☑ Asian Women	2.4		0.8	1.4	1.5		1.2	1.2

Source: Lapchick 2011

Figure 2.1 NCAA Student-Athlete Racial Composition by Selected Sport 2010–2011

Contemporary Racism in Sports: Native American Symbols as Mascots

Native American mascots have remained a common fixture in the world of athletics at all levels from peewee leagues to professional teams. The Washington Redskin has been the mascot of one of the most popular NFL teams, located in our nation's capital, since 1932. The term is considered a disparaging reference to many Native American people. According to Stapleton (2001), "redskin" is a term with a 400-year history and first emerged in sport during a time when the American government actively sought to assimilate Native Americans. In his book *Skull Wars*, Thomas (2000) writes,

> There is today no single word more offensive to Indian people then the term "red-skins," a racial epithet that conjures up the American legacy of bounty hunters bringing in wagon loads of Indian skulls and corpses—literally the bloody dead bodies were known as "redskins"—to collect their payments.
>
> (p. 204)

Although many Native Americans are offended by the term, 88 percent of Americans surveyed oppose a name change for the team (Sigelman 2001).

In a survey of the top 10 most common team mascots, most were birds or beasts of prey, with the exception of two: "Warriors" and "Indians" (Franks 1982). The only two nickname categories that are not predatory animals refer to Native Americans. Many would ask, what's the problem? Are we not honoring indigenous people for being such fierce warriors?

To perceive Native Americans through the eyes of mascots and sports nicknames creates a myopic and inaccurate version of the rich traditions, culture, history, and contemporary existence of the population. Native American mascots are based on the stereotypical "Cowboy and Indian" Wild West images of America's indigenous peoples, with no regard for the diverse cultures and religious beliefs of tribal groups. This manner of stereotyping Native Americans began very early upon European contact. Colonizers portrayed "Indians" as "barbaric," "wild," "bestial," and most of all "savage" (Berkhofer 1978). In fact, Americans' view of "Indians" as predatory beasts has been ingrained from the inception of our nation. George Washington wrote that "Indians" were "wolves and beasts who deserve nothing from whites but total ruin," and President Andrew Jackson stated that troops should seek out "Indians" to "root them out of their dens and kill Indian women and their whelps" (Stannard 1992: 240–41). Racist and dehumanizing descriptions produced mass fear of Native Americans as an entire race or category of people. This fear negates the concept of "honoring" tribes as the basis for naming teams as fierce warriors or other Native American-derived images.

As America grew, these stereotypes were used to justify the systematic genocide of Native Americans, as they were seen as a threat to the safety of colonizers. These images remain a part of American culture, as many Americans continue to visualize the image of a "savage warrior" with feathers and war paint when thinking of Native Americans. One can go into any costume shop and find a Native American costume complete with tomahawk and a feathered headdress. These images have become embraced by **popular culture** and controlled by the **dominant group** instead of Native Americans themselves.

Activism around Native American Imagery

Native American mascots and the use of Native American imagery in advertising and branding (i.e., Land O'Lakes butter, Sue Bee honey, Jeep Cherokee, Crazy Horse Malt Liquor, Winnebagos) grew during the era of racial segregation and legalized discrimination in America (Meerskin 2012). The use of Native American peoples as mascots ranges from generic titles such as Indians, Braves, Warriors, or Savages to specific tribal designations such as Seminoles, Apaches, or Illini. These have been prevalent since the turn of the century, at a time when Little Black Sambo, Frito Bandito, and other racially insensitive branding was commonplace in "less enlightened times" (Graham 1993: 35). While Little Black Sambo and Uncle Rastus have long since been abandoned, the equally insensitive **Chief Wahoo** remains. These images exaggerate physical and cultural aspects of Native Americans and reduce them to one stereotypical representation: savage warrior.

The fight to remove the stereotypical images of Native American mascots and nicknames in sport has been active for nearly four decades. It occurred alongside the **civil rights movement** of the 1960s as the **National Congress of American Indians (NCAI)** began to challenge the use of stereotypical imagery in print and other forms of media (Staurowsky and Baca 2004). The use of Native American mascots also fell under attack when this campaign was launched in 1968. NCAI contended that the use of Native American imagery was not only racist but further reproduced the perception of Native American peoples as sub-human. By 1969 universities began to respond, as Dartmouth College changed its nickname from "the Indians" to "Big Green." Many followed suit, including the universities of Oklahoma, Marquette, and Syracuse, which all dropped Indian nicknames in the 1970s. Currently, an estimated 1,000 academic institutions have relinquished use of Native American mascots or nicknames.

Other institutions have resisted and remain invested in retaining their racist mascots. Close to 1,400 high schools and 70 colleges and universities have refused to cede to calls for change (Staurowsky and Baca 2004). Although Native Americans protest at every home opener with signs that read "We are human beings, not Mascots," MLB's Cleveland Indians maintain the use of the caricatured Chief Wahoo. The Washington Redskins have lost trademark protection, but continue to fight through litigation to maintain the use of the team's mascot. The University of Illinois Fighting Illini fought to maintain their mascot, **Chief Illiniwek**, amid major controversy for over a decade before finally retiring the chief in 2007. The Florida State Seminoles also maintain the use of their Native American imagery, citing an endorsement from the Seminole tribe as justification. All argue that they are honoring the history of Native Americans by using them as mascots. For example, the Cleveland Indians proclaim that the team's designation was chosen to honor the first Native American to play professional baseball, Louis Francis Sockalexis. The University of Illinois argued that their mascot was an honor to the extinct tribe that once inhabited the state. Although Florida State University has been given "permission" to maintain the use of its mascot and nickname by the Seminole tribe and its chief, "there are American Indians protesting outside every Florida State game, including some Seminole people. They say the mascot looks like a Lakota who got lost in an Apache dressing room riding a Nez Perce horse" (Spindel 2002: 16).

Many organizations using Native American designations argue that some Native American individuals and tribal groups have no issue with the use of the mascots and indeed feel a sense of pride. And many fans of these teams agree. In his study of local public opinion, Callais (2010) found that supporters of retaining Native American mascots base their position on maintaining tradition and promoting a color-blind society through a tribute to Native Americans.

While some individual tribes and persons may approve of this practice, all major Native American organizations have denounced it and called for a cessation of the use of their images as mascots, nicknames, and in the branding of products. Mascots are "manufactured images" of Native Americans, and their continued promotion results in a loss of power to control use of those images.

> Indigenous mascots exhibit either idealized or comical facial features and "native" dress, ranging from body-length feathered (usually turkey) headdresses to more subtle fake buckskin attire or skimpy loincloths. Some teams and supporters display counterfeit Indigenous paraphernalia, including tomahawks, feathers, face paints, and symbolic drums and pipes. They also use mock Indigenous behaviors such as the tomahawk chop, dances, chants, drumbeats, war-whooping, and symbolic scalping.
>
> (Pewewardy 1999: 2)

These images were manufactured by their respective schools, universities, and teams. They were created in the minds of those who established them during a time of racial hatred, stereotyping, and when Native Americans were seen as a threat (Callais 2010). The "costumes" of the mascots are derived from stereotypical and widely oversimplified views of a diverse group of people. In reality, each feather and bead, the facial paint, and especially the dances have a distinct, significant, deeply spiritual, and religious meaning to each tribal group. Particular dances mark "the passage of time, the changing of the seasons, a new status in a person's life" and "dancing expresses and consolidates a sense of belonging" (Spindel 2002: 189). In the eyes of many Native Americans, to put on the "costume" and perform a "war dance" at halftime is to mock their religion. How would it go over to have a team designated the "Black Warriors" with a mascot named Chief Watutsi dressed in a loincloth dancing around with a spear? While this mascot would not probably last a single day, Native Americans have been unable to have the use of their images stopped, despite a 40-year struggle to do so.

All in Fun?

Charlene Teters, the Native American activist who called national attention to the University of Illinois fighting Illini, describes how her children reacted when they first witnessed Chief Illiniwek in the documentary *In Whose Honor* (Rosenstein 1997). She describes her son sinking into his chair as he tried to become "invisible." One of the primary arguments against the use of Native American mascots is how it affects children of all races, but especially Native American children. The flippant and inaccurate depiction of Native American culture and identity "causes many young indigenous people to feel shame about who they are as human beings" (Pewewardy 1999: 342). These feelings become a part of the identity and self-image of Native American children, working together with the objective experiences of poverty and deprivation to create low self-esteem and high rates of depression (Pewewardy 1999). One in five Native American youth attempts suicide before the age of 20. In fact, suicide is the second leading cause of death for Native American youth between the ages of 15 and 24 (Center for Native American Youth 2012). This is two and a half times higher than the national average. While there are many factors that contribute to this statistic, such as poverty and drug and alcohol abuse, the use of Native American mascots further damages the self-image of Native American youth. Mascots dehumanize Native Americans and present images, sacred rituals, and other symbols in a way that negates the reverence instilled in Native children, thus negatively impacting their self-esteem. In fact, the American Psychological Association (2001) states emphatically that the use of Native American mascots perpetuates stigmatization of the group and has negative implications for perceptions of self among Native American children and adolescents.

For non-indigenous children, the use of Native American stereotypes as mascots perpetuates the mythical "Cowboys and Indians" view of the group. In a study conducted by Children Now, most of the children studied were found to perceive Native Americans as disconnected from their own way of life (Children Now 1999). Debbie Reese, a Nambe' Pueblo who travels across the country educating children and teachers concerning Native American stereotypes, recounts the many times that children described native people as "exotic," "mythical," or "extinct" and asked if she drove cars or rode horses (Spindel 2002: 224). Most Americans do not come into meaningful contact with traditional Native Americans very often, if at all. Thus, these stereotypical images of mascots and mythical beings are how we learn about Native American culture. Unfortunately, they disallow Americans from visualizing "Indians" as real people, but encourage viewing them as fierce warriors or even clowns dancing around with tomahawks, war paint, and feathered headdresses.

Children and adults alike are profoundly influenced by stereotypical images. The **stereotype threat** is a popular social psychological theory that has been researched empirically since introduced to the literature in 1995 (Steele and Aronson 1995). Claude Steele, a Stanford University professor of social psychology, defines a stereotype threat as "the pressure that a person can feel when she is at risk of confirming, or being seen to confirm a negative stereotype about her group" (Steele and Davies 2003: 311). For instance, when women are reminded that they are women, they perform poorly on math tests due to the stereotype that women are not good at math (Spencer, Steele, and Quinn 1999). Applied to the stereotypical images of Native Americans perpetuated through mascots, these violent and trivialized images may be associated with the lowered self-images of Native youth or the current statistic in which violence accounts for 75 percent of deaths among Native Americans between the ages of 12 and 20 (Center for Native American Youth 2012).

The use of Native American mascots is an example of institutional discrimination. Chief Wahoo and other such images have become as American as baseball itself. They are ingrained into the interworking of our society and its institutions. Major societal institutions such as the economy, sports, and education discriminate against Native Americans by continuing to denigrate living human beings through mascots and team designations. Perhaps if the elite levels of sport (professional and intercollegiate) terminated their use of Native American mascots and raised awareness on the issue, K–12 schools would follow suit. This could serve as an instructional piece for schools as they confront the issue of stereotyping, a process that begins early in one's childhood.

The U.S. Civil Rights Commission released a statement in 2001 condemning the use of Native American mascots. In fact, the National Congress of American Indians, American Indian Movement, National Education Association, National Association for the Advancement of Colored People (NAACP), countless state and local school boards, and the American Psychological Association have all issued similar resolutions. Such images and symbols have been found to perpetuate stereotypes and stigmatization, and negatively affect the mental health and behaviors of Native American people (American Psychological Association 2001). As stated by Native American activist Dennis Banks, "what part of ouch do they not understand?" (Rosenstein 1997).

Conclusion

The issues that Native Americans currently experience in sport—underrepresentation and stereotyping—bring us back to the image of sport as contested terrain. While many believe that the use of Native American mascots is a way of paying tribute, many Native Americans themselves battle to gain more control over the portrayal of their own identity. Athletes are often portrayed as "savages" and "animals," images that Native Americans have fought hard to be disassociated from. And while universities and professional teams generate millions of dollars from the sale of merchandise using Native American imagery, "real" Native Americans remain one of the most impoverished racial groups in society. With a group that experiences disproportionately high rates of dropout, obesity, and suicide, perhaps more effort should be spent on encouraging Native American youth athletics participation, which may help reduce these very problems. Furthermore, their heightened level of participation in sport could also result in society adopting a more positive outlook and understanding of Native Americans, an identification that goes beyond equating Native Americans and sports with mascots.

DISCUSSION QUESTIONS

1. How do you feel about the use of Native American mascots? Do they dishonor Native Americans?

2. Under what circumstances, if any, would it be acceptable to use Caucasian Americans such as the Puritans as sports mascots?

3. What stereotypes exist of a group to which you belong? How would you respond if those stereotypes were used for marketing brands of food, automobiles, or professional sports teams?

4. How can this issue be resolved? Should all teams that have Native American designations be forced to find alternative nicknames or mascots? Why or why not?

III: Hispanics, Béisbol, and the American Dream

Baseball is considered the great American pastime. By the turn of the 20th century, baseball had positioned itself as a part of the American identity and as a repository of "national values" (Iber et al. 2011: 78). It is called "America's game" and considered as "American as apple pie." Embedded within the history of baseball is a complex story of race and race relations. Jackie Robinson is synonymous with the integration of baseball, but Hispanic and Native American players actually entered baseball long before Blacks.

During the era of Jim Crow racial segregation, Spanish-speaking Latinos in baseball "blurred any line between inclusion and exclusion, racial eligibility and ineligibility" (Burgos 2007: 4). Sports mirror the larger society, and Hispanics are often considered the "other" minority in American society. The term "Hispanic" was introduced into the U.S. census in 1970 and was a way to count individuals who had a relationship to Spain. Today the term includes "a person of Cuban, Mexican, Puerto Rican, South or Central American, or other Spanish culture or origin regardless of race" (U.S. Census Bureau 2010). It has come to be used as an elastic term, an umbrella that includes groups from diverse national, geographic, and cultural origins.

During the last three decades the Hispanic population in the United States has grown rapidly. In the 2010 census, 50.5 million or 16 percent of the U.S. population self-identified as Hispanic or Latino (U.S. Census Bureau 2010). This was a 3.8 percent increase from the 2000 Census. Hispanics have begun to enter the discussion on race that was primarily focused on the Black/White dichotomy in the United States. Much of what we know about Hispanic participation in baseball is restricted to elite levels of participation, particularly Major League Baseball.

While there has been a 218 percent increase in Hispanic Major Leaguers over the past 20 years, Hispanics have been a rich part of the history of the game since the late 1800s (Ortiz 2011). Of the 16 teams, 13 had at least one Hispanic player prior to Jackie Robinson's baseball debut in 1947 (Burgos 2007). The success of Cuban players such as Armando Marsans and Rafael Almeida, who played for the Cincinnati Reds in 1911, helped spread the game to Puerto Rico and the Dominican Republic in the early to mid-1900s. Around 1920, American oil workers took the sport to Venezuela (Harkins 2012). While some **Black Latinos** such as Cubans Orestes Minoso and Alejandro Pompez were successful in baseball's **Negro Leagues**, a few were able to gain access to the White leagues by overemphasizing their Spanish accents in order to separate themselves from English-speaking U.S. Black players (Burgos 2009).

Hispanic players once perceived baseball as a means to assimilate, to become "more American." However, the growth of Hispanic players in the MLB now appears to reinforce a sense of cultural identity and pride for this rapidly growing ethnic group. With the celebrated successes of Los Angeles Dodgers pitcher Fernando Valenzuela in the 1980s and Sammy Sosa in the 1990s, Spanish speakers began to identify more fully with the success of Latino superstars in Major League Baseball.

Naturals: Hispanics and Socialization into Baseball

At the start of the 2011 season, 27 percent of Major Leaguers and approximately 42 percent of Minor League baseball players were Hispanic (Keown 2011). More specifically, 10 percent of the MLB players were from the tiny island of the Dominican Republic (Harkins 2012). While White players disproportionately represent Major Leaguers, both White and Black players are declining in numbers as league managers and team owners heavily invest in player development and baseball academies in the Americas, including Central America and the Caribbean. Figure 3.1 shows the growth of Hispanic Major League players over the past 20 years, as well as the decline of White and Black players.

Lou Melendez, MLB's vice president for international baseball operations, referenced the "tremendous investments in Latin America" as the source of continued growth in the number of Latin American players (Harkins 2012: 2). Many have begun

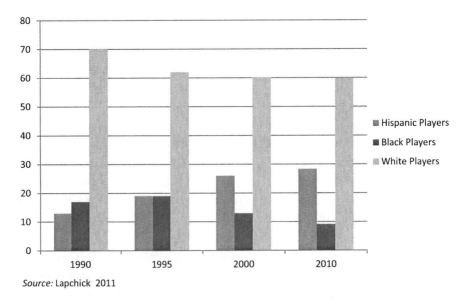

Source: Lapchick 2011

Figure 3.1 Hispanic, White, and Black Players in Major League Baseball 1990–2010

to look at Major League Baseball and ask very specific questions about why Hispanic baseball players are becoming so prevalent in the major leagues.

Most discussion has centered on the growth of Hispanics in the United States as a whole, and whether that growth would naturally produce more Hispanic baseball players. However, some Americans seem to believe that Hispanics are simply naturally better at baseball than other racial/ethnic groups. This age-old discussion of natural athletic gifts within racial/ethnic groups is deeply rooted in stereotyping. Blacks are overrepresented in football, basketball, and the sprinting and jumping events in track and field, giving birth to the common sentiment that they are naturally better athletes in those areas. Some factions believe that Africans who long ago survived treacherous trips to the Americas were the healthiest and fittest of the travelers, and that today's athletes are descendants of those individuals—or that Black slaves in America were bred to be larger and stronger, thereby producing athletic superiority of slave descendants (Sailes 1991). This tendency to attribute athleticism to skin color or group membership is common and reflects **prejudice** and an inclination toward stereotyping, regardless of the population to which it is applied.

With the "Fernandomania" that resulted from the overwhelming success of Dodgers pitcher Fernando Valenzuela in the 1980s, sports managers began to believe that this same success could be replicated by finding more players who looked like Valenzuela—again attributing ability to group membership (Iber et al. 2011). However, this type of thinking is just as much a fallacy in the case of Hispanic players as it is in Black athlete stereotyping. We often ask our students if they think Blacks are better athletes and frequently receive an overwhelming and emphatic "*YES*," as they name countless examples of amazing Black athletes. But the same students have difficulty explaining the "natural" success among Whites in other sports such as tennis, hockey, gymnastics, and others. After all, these sports are predominantly made up of White athletes at all levels of athletic participation.

The range of natural athletic abilities such as size, speed, agility, and coordination is similar across racial groups. There is more variation within groups than between groups. What creates the overrepresentation of racial groups in certain sports is quite simply socialization and economics. The "notion of natural athlete no doubt applies primarily to people who are born with physical attributes such as coordination … however, the refinement of these attributes … as well as the physiological aspects of play, sport, and athletics have to be acquired" (Snyder and Spreitzer 1978: 55). Socialization into sports is a process associated with agents or agencies that are influential in attracting children to sports and includes the learning of social, psychological, and physical skills needed in athletic involvement (Snyder and Spreitzer 1978). Some of the socializing factors are family, peers, community, schools, and the mass media. Children learn at an early age the importance of sports in society from media, parents, and friends, and these agents of socialization are also critical factors in determining *which* sport a child will play. For instance, in his study of baseball players, Hill (1993) found that high school coaches were very influential in a youth's decision to focus exclusively on baseball. Physical scientists have the ability to describe physical differences between athletes and non-athletes, and social scientists answer why some individuals are involved in particular athletic roles and why some athletes ascend to elite levels of performance.

Black young men are bombarded with media images, and at the same time familial and neighborhood socialization often emphasizes football and basketball as avenues for success. Hispanic baseball players are inundated with images of baseball players who give that same message. Sailes (1991) found that socialization patterns such as a lack of Black role models outside of sports, absence of facilities, and institutionalized racism keep Black athletes out of some sports and cause overrepresentation in other sports. Hispanic baseball players who show any promise in the Americas including Central America and the Caribbean are funneled into a system that develops them for ultimate success in the sport. Hispanics experienced the growth of Spanish surnames on the diamond and began modeling that behavior, focusing on baseball in a similar manner to how Black males focus on basketball and football. It is not only a result of the growth in the Hispanic population in America that explains why the MLB has had a 218 percent increase in Hispanic players—if that were the case we would see similar growth patterns in all sports, including football and basketball.

Hispanic players in the Americas including Central America and the Caribbean focus on becoming great baseball players at a very young age. With an annual average per capita income of $5,200 in the Dominican Republic, the lure of sports success, no matter how meager by American standards, is overwhelming for Dominican boys. Major League Baseball is composed of around 25 percent Hispanic players, 10 percent of which are Dominican (Ortiz 2011). Baseball has become the most visible, and in the eyes of Dominican boys, the most accessible means to escape the dismal future of poverty and lack of opportunity in the Dominican Republic.

The **social imitation theory** describes the socialization process based on the notion of vicarious learning. The theory maintains that individuals are passive in the socialization process and learn by observing and modeling the behaviors of **reference groups** and socializing agents, such as family, peers, and media. More importantly, individuals can base their desires and career aspirations on the outcomes of those they are modeling. This theory has been applied when explaining the overemphasis on sport among Black males in the United States as they vicariously learn that sports produce positive consequences, such as a lucrative professional career (McPherson, Curtis, and Loy 1989). Similarly, Hispanics see baseball as a viable means toward upward economic and **social mobility**. Baseball is seen as their shot at the "American Dream" as they model the behavior of professional baseball players. No place else in the American media can Hispanic boys see themselves represented in a positive way on such a wide scale. This, together with MLB's investment in baseball academies in the Americas including Central America and the Caribbean, creates a myopic view of baseball as a means to exit the poverty in their home country and an opportunity for a better life in the United States. Role models such as Eddie Perez from Venezuela, who came to the United States at 17 on a professional contract with the Atlanta Braves and went on to a successful career as a player and coach, breathe life into this dream (Harkins 2012). Additionally, folklore and sensational stories add to the mystique of sports, such as players making gloves out of milk cartons in the Dominican Republic; or those such as Jaime Navarro, a Puerto Rican who pitched 12 years in the MLB, describing bats made from tree branches. These stories appeal to the belief in the possibilities of hard work and determination leading to rags-to-riches lives. The results are socialization patterns that center on baseball and ultimately the development and sharpening of the physical, psychological, and technical skills to succeed in that particular sport. Similarly, Hispanic American children identify with the success of Spanish speakers in the sport and model the behavior of that reference group. If these factors continue, Hispanics will become increasingly overrepresented in professional baseball, much like Blacks are overrepresented in football and basketball for similar reasons.

Implications: Anti-Immigrant Sentiment?

Anti-immigration sentiments continue to burgeon in the United States. Illegal immigration is seen as a threat to American nationalism, and undocumented immigrants are used as scapegoats for unemployment, crime, and other social ills. Controversial anti-immigration laws in states such as Georgia, Arizona, Alabama, and others illustrate the fear of Hispanic immigration and the stereotyping of Hispanics as "illegal avengers." Protestors call for lawmakers to deport illegal immigrants and deny their children the benefits of American citizenship. Sports are a reflection of society, so are we seeing that same sentiment brewing in baseball?

Around 62 percent of Hispanic Americans surveyed claimed to be baseball fans, while 59 percent of the total population considered themselves to be fans of the game (ESPN 2011). Additionally, Hispanics are approximately 33 percent more likely to attend MLB games than the general population. For this reason, the growth in Hispanic presence is seen as a benefit to the economy, and Hispanics are being directly marketed to as a target audience. On the other hand, articles such as "Is Major League Baseball too Hispanic?" featured on ESPN.com (Keown 2011) and "Is baseball turning into Latin America's game?" (Harkins 2012), as well as discussion on sport radio and talk shows, illustrate that Americans are not thrilled about the game becoming less "American." For instance, Klein's (2000) study involving the Boston Red Sox showed how the team and local media used their star pitcher at the time, Pedro Martinez, to market baseball to the Latino community. Though Fenway quickly attracted more Hispanic fans, his interviews with White fans suggested that Anglos viewed the recent integration more negatively. Nevertheless, baseball has always been and still largely continues to be lacking in diversity at the youth and local level. Expensive **select** programs, private coaches, and travel have kept the sport mostly populated by upper middle-class Whites (Farry 2008).

The fear that Latinos or Hispanics are taking over America's game is fueled by the "mentality that good old American ball players are getting squeezed out by Latin players" (Keown 2011: 2). This fear may have been what prompted the new labor agreement which caps the spending on international players at $3 million annually (Quinn 2012). The agreement will essentially slow down the flow of Dominican and Venezuelan players (Puerto Rican players are domestic), and greatly decrease their earning potential. Why would such an agreement be necessary if not to limit the growth of brown players on the diamond? As a reflection of larger society, baseball seems to be following suit with anti-immigrant sentiment and the fear that immigrant population growth is in some way a threat to the American way of life, including its favorite pastimes.

Conclusion

Our view of race and sport as contested terrain applies to the issues presented in this chapter on Hispanics and baseball. As we've emphasized, sport provides opportunities for success that many minorities might not otherwise experience. But as opportunities have increased for Hispanic players across the world to integrate into professional baseball, American society has responded by questioning whether the sport is becoming *too* Hispanic, a debate which has underpinnings in a larger discussion on immigration in America.

This debate can be seen through the more complex story of Danny Almonte, a Dominican immigrant and Little League baseball star who, like many Dominican males, immigrated to the United States with the hope of using baseball as a means to upward mobility. Almonte was an "almost All-American hero" (King-White 2010: 186); his team made it to the Little League World Series where his pitching performance dominated opposing batters. Almonte was a "hero" and symbol of immigrant success. However, this status abruptly changed when, shortly after the World Series ended, it was discovered that he was 14, two years older than the Little League permits. Suddenly, Almonte became a symbol of an assault by immigrants on White interests. Almonte was no longer portrayed as an American, but as a Dominican immigrant and a cheat (King-White 2010).

Almonte aside, the United States has witnessed the success of many Hispanic athletes at elite levels; however, the successes of few sometimes blind us to the struggles of many. Few Hispanics across the world actually enter the Major League ranks as players, and even fewer make their way into more long-term or executive positions. Still, the demographic make-up of the MLB has dramatically shifted to include a heavy presence of Hispanics. This has important implications for issues of race and sport. As we discuss in the context of Blacks in the next chapter, the overrepresentation of minorities in certain sports can have both positive and negative consequences. Positively, it reveals more progress toward integration and opportunities for success. Negatively, the overrepresentation of minority groups in certain sports perpetuates and exacerbates myths of race and the notion that some groups have "natural" talent, thereby ignoring the role of socialization in producing these outcomes. Additionally, as we have highlighted in this chapter, reducing overrepresentation to myths about natural talent ignores the exploitative efforts made by executives to secure cheaper labor.

DISCUSSION QUESTIONS

1. What factors contribute to the racial/ethnic segregation that is seen in sports?
2. Why do some Americans appear to fear the rapid growth of the Hispanic population?
3. Do you agree with the argument that some groups are simply better suited physically for success in specific sports? Explain the limitations and problems with this argument.

IV: Black Athletics: Golden Opportunity?

In 1936, as Hitler anticipated that the Berlin Olympic Games would be a platform for showcasing the superiority of Aryan peoples, Black track and field athlete Jesse Owens denied him that opportunity. Owens won four gold medals and handily defeated Hitler's Aryan athletes. The Olympic Games of 1936 were considered by many to be a victory of democracy over Nazism. Similarly, the 1938 victory of the Black boxer, Joe Louis, over the German Max Schmeling is viewed by sport historians as a critical moment in the history of race and sport in America (Randolph Sugar 2006). These individualistic feats, as well as the increased presence and success of Black college athletes across the North, were part of and reflected a shift in attitudes among Whites toward Blacks (Spivey 1983).

In 1947, Jackie Robinson, who is now celebrated as champion for integration and civil rights, broke the color line to become the first Black to play professional baseball, signing with the Brooklyn Dodgers. Robinson represented a shift in the dominant racial **paradigm.** In 1942, Robinson fought to be accepted into the Army's Officer Candidate School and was at first denied because of his race (Robinson 1995). After protest, he was admitted into officer training. Although Robinson himself was never deployed, his unit became one of the first all-Black battalions to fight in World War II (Robinson 1995). The shift in thought pattern amongst Americans concerning Blacks led to the push toward racial integration and was inspired in part by Black soldiers who fought bravely along with Whites during the war.

The success of all Black units such as the Tuskegee Airmen who flew over 200 successful missions, never losing a bomber to enemy fire, forced mainstream America to reexamine their negative assessments of Blacks and their capabilities to contribute to society (Scott and Womack 1992). Black soldiers' service in World War II was symbolized by the "Double V" or two victories (Scott and Womack 1992). As stated by U.S. Army Colonel Bill De Shields, a historian and founder of the Black Military History Institute of America, the Double V represented "Victory against the enemy abroad, and victory against the enemy at home. The enemy at home of course being racism, discrimination, prejudice and Jim Crow" (Voice of America 2009). Jim Crow—state segregation of housing, education, and other institutions and public spheres—was a way of life in America from 1876 until the 1970s. Over one million Black soldiers fought in World War II and it is no coincidence that an Army veteran, Robinson, forced America to view integration in a new light.

Over the next several decades we began to see many "firsts." Willie O'Ree became the first Black to play in the National Hockey League (NHL) in 1958 and in 1963 Arthur Ashe became the first Black to be selected for the United States Davis Cup team in tennis (Lapchick 2008). These firsts in the sporting world became examples for racial integration in America as a whole. As Black athletes began to populate some of America's favorite sports, fans began to look at race in a different way. They were now cheering for people with black and brown skin as representatives of their favorite sports teams. Black and White teammates worked side by side toward a common goal and on common ground, breaking down the prejudices of both groups.

There is no doubt that Black sport participation has been positive for the group and for American society as a whole. However, contemporarily, there are two divergent views concerning Black males in athletics. The first perspective is that sports are a "golden opportunity," or a way out of less than desirable economic and social situations. Sports, from this perspective, provide a way to circumvent the many perceived and actual barriers to success for Black males. The opposing view is that the overemphasis on sports amongst Black males is, in fact, one of those barriers that prevent the social and economic mobility of the group. From this perspective, Black men are mesmerized by the lure of sports fame and fortune, while being distracted from other occupations that hold far greater promise for economic mobility and escalation of social status. A tragedy of sorts:

> Triple tragedy … One, the tragedy of thousands upon thousands of Black youths in the obsessive pursuit of sports goals that the overwhelming majority of them will never attain. Two, the tragedy of the personal and cultural underdevelopment that afflicts so many successful and unsuccessful Black sports aspirants. Three, the tragedy of cultural and institutional underdevelopment throughout Black society as a consequence of the drain in talent potential toward sports and away from other vital areas of occupational and career emphasis such as medicine, law, economics, politics, education, and technical fields.
>
> (Harrison 2000: 36)

The triple tragedy that Harrison alludes to is essentially an opportunity cost for both individuals and society. In comparison to their White counterparts, Black males are socialized by family and communities into certain sports, thereby limiting their exposure to other career paths and **role models**, and pushing sports as a promising career early in life (Beamon 2008; Beamon and Bell 2002, 2006; Edwards 2000; Harris 1994). As seen in Figure 4.1, the funnel to professional sports is extremely narrow.

More specifically, out of every 40,000 Black basketball players, 35 will play in the

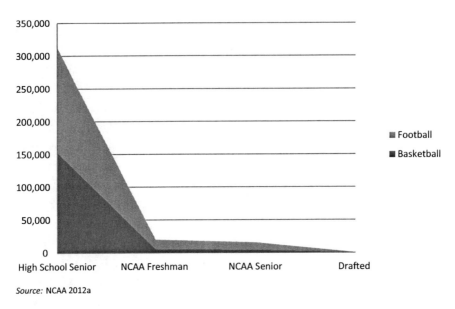

Source: NCAA 2012a

Figure 4.1 Path to Professional Football and Basketball

NBA and only seven will be starters (Eitzen 2003). There are around 30,015 Black physicians and 30,800 Black lawyers, and fewer than 3,500 Black professional athletes in all sports combined (Coakley 2010). However, for many Black student athletes, their belief in a professional sports career is very salient and undeterred by these facts. During an interview conducted for previous research, one former athlete stated to the first author:

> … it wasn't a dream, it was real, it was … understood. Never once did I see it as a dream, a dream is something that you think about that may not come true. This was a reality. I mean at twelve it was pro football, later pro basketball, so maybe I didn't know what sport I would go pro in, but I knew I was going to play pro ball. It was always a reality.

Sports participation can be beneficial to youth in many ways. In fact, among Black boys, youth sports have been shown to increase academic success, reduce delinquency, and improve self-concept (Braddock 1991; Melnick, Sabo, and Vanfossen 1992; Jordan 1999). However, studies also show that while sports can be a resource for Black male youth for the aforementioned reasons, the significance is lower than for other groups, and those focusing on football and basketball had even lower gains associated with youth and adolescent sports participation (Eitle and Eitle 2002; Jordan 1999). In fact, Black males playing football and basketball actually had lower performance on standardized tests than other groups (Eitle and Eitle 2002). Additionally, intense focus upon sports as a future career can have negative consequences that disallow this group to benefit fully from the pro-social outcomes normally associated with youth sports. Overemphasizing athletic participation during childhood produces lower levels of academic achievement, higher expectations for professional sports careers as a means to upward mobility and economic success, dependence on athletic identities, lower levels of **career maturity**, and lower levels of life satisfaction after sports retirement for elite and collegiate athletes (Adler and Adler 1991; Beamon 2008, 2010). As the targets of much of this socialization, Black males experience these negative effects disproportionately. Moreover, due to the increasing presence of youth sport camps that are organized around age, height, and weight (and often unintentionally, race), children's abilities and potential for other choices and opportunities have been stifled as they get pigeonholed into certain sports and points at younger and younger periods in life (Edwards 2010).

The impact of popular culture's image of the Black male athlete on their behavior and life chances has been examined by scholars and social activists for decades. Many studies evaluate the effects of this image on the career aspirations, academic performance, and self-concepts of young Black males. Harry Edwards, a leading sport sociologist and activist, argues that the push toward athletics in Black families hinders the social and cognitive growth of Black youth (Edwards 2000). Exceptional athletes such as Lebron "King" James, Michael Jordan, and Emmitt Smith are household names, but the failures of many others are unrecognized. In addition, images of successful Black athletes abound, but there are few images of successful Black men in other fields to counterbalance them. The number of Black male public role models who are successful in business or education are few and far between, which perpetuates the stereotype that Black males are primarily or even exclusively athletically talented (Hoberman 1997). And according to Edwards (2010), even the type of role model has changed among Black athletes. During the civil rights era, athletes such as Jim Brown and Muhammad Ali were also activists and promoters of racial advancement and equality. Edwards argues that contemporary Black athletes have experienced "modeling reversal" and aspire to be "real," "authentic," and create an image of "street cred," which can have deleterious consequences for youth in the search for role models.

Controversy surrounds Black males in competitive athletics, especially when connected with educational institutions. Many assert that "over-identification with athletes and the world of physical performances limits the development of Black children by discouraging academic achievement in favor of physical expression" (Hoberman 2000: 5). Schools and universities prepare students for futures beyond their walls by providing access to the tools to experience upward mobility. Although participation in athletics is often considered a golden opportunity for Blacks, compelling evidence to the contrary has been presented for decades. In one study of Division I football players in a major conference, 85 percent of Black players had expectations to play in the NFL as opposed to 39 percent of White players (Beamon and Bell 2002). Beliefs about professional sports opportunities have both direct and indirect consequences for student-athletes' academic performance. If a student-athlete views his sport as his most viable route to economic success, he will give most of his effort and concentration to his sport, often minimizing the importance of his academic achievement (Beamon and Bell 2002).

Dilemmas in Collegiate Athletics

Academic Difficulties

Over time, the relationship between sports and education has become less than symbiotic. Universities commercialize their sports programs for revenue, increased visibility, recruitment of students, and increased alumni support. These goals put tremendous pressure to win on student-athletes (Donnor 2005; Upthegrove, Roscigno, and Charles 1999). Due to their ability to raise a university's profile and add to the profitability of athletic programs, exceptional athletes are highly valued by universities. As a result of overrepresentation among Blacks in **revenue-generating sports**, it has been estimated that Black student-athletes competing for universities have earned more than a quarter of a trillion dollars for their universities over a 40-year period; some argue that this money has been effectively transferred out of the Black community (NCAA 2006b; Salome 2005). The exploitation of student-athletes for their athletic abilities is a possible consequence of revenue-generating expectations placed on universities. The demand for top-quality athletes to elevate team performance and produce revenue may cause universities to neglect their educational responsibilities to the student-athletes. Contradictory pressures are placed on student-athletes in their role as students. There is a clear emphasis placed upon the physical capabilities of student-athletes, and consequently their academic abilities and roles as students are often overlooked and underemphasized (Hawkins 1999; Litsky 2003; Maloney and McCormick 1993; Eitzen 2000, 2003). Sack and Staurowsky (1998) discuss the exploitation of student-athletes, stating, "Universities are far more concerned with exploiting the athletic talent [of student-athletes] than with nurturing academic potential" (p. 104).

Although Black student-athletes graduate at a higher rate than non-athlete Black students, the disparity between White and Black athletes' graduation rates is considerable. In Division I football, White players graduate at a 20 percent higher rate than Black players; in Division I basketball, the gap is widening and is now at 32 percent (Lapchick 2011). Black male student-athletes at Division I-A universities have the lowest graduation rate of all racial, ethnic, and gender classifications (Smith 2004). Ironically, some of the most successful athletic programs in the country have the lowest levels of academic success among Black student-athletes. In a national study, student-athletes reported feeling that athletic departments were more concerned with maintaining their eligibility than promoting the pursuit of a meaningful education (Sailes 1998). It is common for any reference to education by coaches or counselors to be made in terms of eligibility. One athlete from an elite football program said:

...the name of the game is to stay eligible, ya know what I'm saying. I guess in the recruitment process, when a coach or whoever is representing that university is sitting in front of your parents uh, academics is stressed highly. However when you get there, that is not the case.

(Beamon 2008: 356)

Many athletes report that the term "student-athlete" is not descriptive of the demands placed on them. A student-athlete stated:

I mean, they drill on you going to class and making the grade, but that's only because if you don't go to class and make the grade, then you can't be on the field. ... Student-athlete, that's not how it is, it's athletic-student. It's backwards for college athletics.

(Beamon 2008: 357)

For many university student-athletes in revenue-generating sports, regardless of race, academic and cognitive development is frequently hindered by athletic training and travel. Student-athletes often find it difficult to balance athletics, academics, and social roles. Athletes have less time available for the educational process that "extends beyond going to class every day to socializing with research and study groups, participating with student organizations, and attending campus activities apart from athletics" (Hawkins 1999: 8). Additionally, due to mental and physical exhaustion from sports participation that is often equivalent to a full work week, student-athletes have decreased levels of energy and attention to study and complete assignments. Given this heavy workload, it is difficult for some student-athletes to benefit from assistance that may be available, such as tutoring programs and counseling. In addition to burn-out and fatigue, athletes often experience significant scheduling conflicts (Person, Benson-Quaziena, and Rogers 2001; Beamon and Bell 2002). A former starter at a big-time college football program discusses the term "student-athlete" as:

...they tell you, you a student first and an athlete next, but really you an athlete first and a student second. There is more emphasis on making your practices and meetings. They hit you with the go to class and all that stuff, but they don't care. As long as they get them four years out of you they could care less if you get a degree or not ... I think they have to [care about athletes getting degrees] cuz they job depends somewhat on it, but personally, I don't think they care.

(Beamon 2008: 356)

Black males are seen as particularly vulnerable to these circumstances since they often enter college with other background disadvantages (e.g., socioeconomic status, academic preparedness) and **goal discrepancy** concerning professional sports careers (Roscigno 1999; Sellers and Kuperminc 1997). They are easy targets for exploitation because their expectations for professional sports careers have been reinforced by parents, coaches, and the media. Thus, they will often sacrifice academic success and career preparation outside of sports to please coaches and perform to their maximum athletic potential. It is easier for colleges to get the most out of these indoctrinated athletes, leading to a better conditioned, highly focused, and more prepared team. This, undoubtedly, leads to winning and greater rewards for the university. However, it leads to a lower quality of education, lower probability of earning a degree, and lowered level of career-preparedness for Black student-athletes.

The consequences for Black student-athletes are severe in comparison to their White counterparts due to an underlying pattern of racism in college sports and in society as a whole. Eitzen (2000) presents several problems related to the exploitation of Black student-athletes: lack of preparation for college courses, isolation, lack of Blacks in leadership positions in athletic departments, and stereotypes held by professors and members of athletic departments. The noted lack of Black coaches, administrators, managers, and owners was outlined in Chapter 1. These factors "exploit the talent of Black athletes and deny these same athletes access to a quality education" as well as limit "employment opportunities of Black athletes after their career ends" (Meggyesy 2000: 27). Hawkins (1999) concludes that Black student-athletes are victims of labor exploitation due to the fact that the universities are the only areas to "contract their talents" (p. 7). Additionally, the revenue-generating sports that are largely Black fund the non-revenue-generating sports (golf, tennis, swimming, gymnastics, etc.) that are almost exclusively White. Which, in fact, is quite ironic considering that these non-revenue sports are generally populated by upper-middle- and upper-class participants, as these sports are expensive and generally not accessible to working-class and middle-class families at the youth and local level; yet they are almost fully supported by football and basketball (lower-class) sports at the elite college level.

Inadequate Career Preparation

While student-athletes may fulfill their obligation to schools by performing athletically and bringing recognition to the institution, all too often they do not see the benefits of their labor by going on to play professionally or by earning a degree that leads to successful careers. One of the major consequences of the overemphasis placed on sports by Black young men is a lack of career maturity. One of the primary sources of career immaturity among college athletes comes from choosing their major. Of those who graduate, a large proportion of Black student-athletes graduate in areas that are less marketable, such as majors that are "riddled with 'keep 'em eligible,' less competitive 'jock courses' of dubious educational value and occupational relevance" (Edwards 1988: 138). Student-athletes cannot choose majors with required courses held during times set aside for practice and meetings (e.g., majors like architecture or sciences, which often have afternoon labs). Athletes in previous research discuss

being encouraged to choose majors with courses considered "easy to pass" or departments that were "athlete friendly." For these reasons and to remain eligible, they often
develop educational goals that are compatible with athletic participation as opposed to
ones that place them on an effective career path. Devin, a business major, had a desire
to become an engineer. He ended up in a major that he was far less interested in:

> My major was something I just kinda wind up getting, I started off wanting to be
> an engineer, but it's like the labs and stuff would conflict with practice. And cuz I
> was on scholarship, they figured, uh, my football stuff was more important than
> going to class or being what I truly wanted to be, so I kinda fell into my degree.
>
> (Beamon 2008: 360)

Many of the athletes in previous studies have found themselves in a similar situation.
For example, another respondent stated:

> Initially when I first went to college I wanted to major in psychology. But because
> my, um, the classes for my major were going to conflict with football practice.
> So I was not allowed to choose those classes … so instead of psychology I chose
> journalism.
>
> (ibid.)

Many student-athletes the first author has interviewed expressed a sense of exploitation by the university. One respondent summarized the perception of many by noting
that after four years of eligibility the sentiment was: "Okay we've used you up now so
good-bye and good luck to ya and don't come back around here no more." They felt ill-
prepared for choosing a viable career path after their sports careers ended because the
major programs, which they felt pushed into, did not necessarily connect to their abilities or desires for a future career. When asked if individual athletes benefited equally
with universities from college athletic programs, most believed the university reaped
more rewards. For example, a football player from a major football powerhouse stated:

> …the colleges make so much money off of the athletes … those athletes are pro-
> ducing those winning records and those winning records are producing millions
> for that college but the athletes don't see any of that, and they get away with it by
> saying "well ok we're giving you a free education.
>
> (Beamon 2008: 358)

Racism on Campus

Black male football and basketball players are not protected from racism by their
status as high-profile athletes in the big-time sports programs at Division I-A universities. In fact, they may have an even more difficult experience with racism on campus

than non-athletes. Black student-athletes have discussed in research studies that they have been forbidden to speak out against racism by coaches and athletic departments, which at times detached them from their non-athlete counterparts (Lapchick 1996). This type of restriction may further feelings of isolation and, as one student-athlete stated, make them feel like a "sell-out." However, like other Black students at **predominately White institutions (PWIs),** many student-athletes feel racial isolation as the result of being one of few Black students on campus (Altbach 1991; Feagin and Sikes 1995; Smith, Allen, and Danley 2007). These student-athletes encounter a great deal of face-to-face individual racism through name-calling by fans and other students. Fans can feel a sense of entitlement and may not hesitate to use racial descriptions, as well as racial epithets, to insult athletes when they fall short in competition. As one Black student-athlete recalled, "The first time I *ever* got called a nigger was by a fan." Another stated, "I had a fan yell out 'you sorry nigger' after I missed an easy catch, they loved me when I was winning, but I was a 'nigger' when I messed up" (Beamon forthcoming).

In regard to Black student-athletes, there are two primary opposing perspectives about the role of collegiate sports in the lives of individuals: (1) athletics provides educational opportunities to Blacks from underprivileged backgrounds that they would not otherwise have, and (2) involvement with sports has exploited Black athletes (Sellers 2000). Although many people believe that high-profile athletes in big-time athletic programs are in many ways given special treatment, respondents in previous research discussed feeling mistreated and stereotyped while in college. For example, one student-athlete discussed his experiences in the classroom, and denoted that racism "is a part of everyday life":

> ...in the classroom they made a racist statement in which I was the only African-American in the classroom and they tend to forget that I was in there, and once they realized I was in there everybody face turn red and I had a whole lot of apologies. But ya know, that's a part of life, you have to accept it and move on.
>
> (Beamon forthcoming)

Black student-athletes at PWIs often experience the overwhelming stereotype that they are there based solely on athletic talents (Feagin and Sikes 1995; Harrison and Lawrence 2003). One of the most common stereotypes of Black males is that they have innate athletic superiority (Hall 2001; Lapchick 1996). This stereotype, coupled with the "dumb jock" stereotype applied generally to student-athletes, creates a double jeopardy of sorts for Black athletes on campus.

Conclusion

Athletics has in fact been a golden opportunity for many Blacks who otherwise might not have attended college. As we argued earlier (see Chapter I), sports can be perceived as an avenue of escape from the "ghetto" or a means of circumventing perceived discrimination in U.S. society (Hartmann 2000). However, the socialization of Blacks into sports such as football and basketball can also mean a one-track pursuit of success at a critical period in teenagers' lives. While education provides a much more realistic means to achievement, it is often abandoned, or at least minimized.

For the proportionate few who do earn scholarships, it can be argued that Black talents are exploited by universities. However, one could also argue that the Black community should begin to see sports differently, and try harder to combat the "innate athletic superiority" myth by deliberately and intensively developing other talents and pushing toward other worthy career paths so that, for example, it is a more common aspiration for a Black male to become a neurosurgeon than an NBA player. Although the media do not present diverse images, it is the responsibility of universities, families, and even coaches to promote academic, career, and cognitive growth outside of sports.

The current issues that Blacks experience uniquely in the social institution of sport reveal contested terrain. On one hand, sport has afforded Black Americans means to success. Also, many types of sports have become increasingly integrated, suggesting a growing acceptance toward people of color in one of America's most consumed areas of leisure. On the other hand, Blacks are so overrepresented as players in sports such as football and basketball that scholars have begun to question if this leads to unrealistic expectations among the millions of children who will not make it to professional levels of sport or even earn scholarships as student-athletes at universities.

DISCUSSION QUESTIONS

1. Do universities take advantage of student-athletes and—in a sense—exploit their talents?
2. Do you think that U.S. Blacks place more emphasis upon sports, when compared to other groups? Is this problem more widespread across racial and ethnic lines?
3. What can universities do to deemphasize sports and provide other career options for student-athletes?

V: When the Crowd Stops Cheering: Negotiating the Transition

W hat happens to elite athletes who have focused solely on athletics as a means to success upon retirement from sport? Do Black male athletes convert gains made through athletic accomplishments to cultural and social capital and financial success post sports? The average professional sports career lasts between three and five years (Coakley 2010), which means that most professional athletes will retire from sports careers before age 30. In an interview with a former professional football player, the 27-year-old "retiree" discussed his transition into the workforce:

> It was literally unbelievable ... it's like losing your left leg or one of your arms or something cuz it's something you've had all your life, it's been in your life all your life as far as you can remember and it's just gone ... Sports have been as much a part of my life as my parents, and it's just taken away like that ... I had a degree, but it wasn't in anything I wanted to do and I really didn't really know how to go get a career started. I didn't make enough money when I was playing to really take care of my family so I just had to go from job to job. Making like minimum wage and I even had a degree and everything, I just didn't know how to make it work for me. It was tough, I mean I probably went through six or seven jobs in a year. Ya know ... I had no experience at anything. I couldn't work in college, couldn't really do no internships in college ... so I was basically in a pickle, I didn't know what I was gone do. So I just started picking up jobs wherever I could.
> (Beamon and Bell 2011: 34, 37; Beamon and Messer forthcoming)

Another former NFL player, retired by 27, discussed how sports hindered his transition into the work world after retirement:

> That was the only thing they were really worried about and that was the only conversation they really would have with me, about the athletics ... it seemed like that was what the majority of the conversations was consumed with ... it caused problems later on and after I began my career outside of sports that's the only thing they wanna talk about. I had a problem with that ... Ya know if you're gonna interview me for a job and you asking about sports, you won't get to know

about me and my capabilities, you'll just know about the sports. And a lot of times you don't get the job because they don't have anything down good about you, about the capabilities that you can do on that job, all they know is about sports.

(Beamon 2012: 204)

Retirement presents difficulties for all elite athletes; however, for many Black athletes the transition to retirement can present additional issues. Like other male athletes, they have been socialized to perceive sports as the most viable avenue to social mobility and economic security. Even for those who do play in the NFL, NBA, or other semiprofessional and professional outlets, sports careers are fairly short-lived in most instances and former elite athletes are ill-prepared for life after retirement. Obtaining large, financially lucrative contracts though doesn't guarantee a life of economic security either (Matthews 2010). Rick Reilly (2008), a prominent writer for ESPN, reports that nearly 60 percent of NBA players are broke only five years after retiring, primarily due to wasteful spending. For instance, Latrell Sprewell earned nearly $50 million during his career and filed for bankruptcy in 2007; Kenny Anderson filed for bankruptcy after earning $60 million; Derrick Coleman lost nearly $87 million before filing; and Scottie Pippen filed for bankruptcy after earning $120 million.

Retirement can lead to a sudden realization that an individual's athletic development was more important to themselves, their families, and coaches than the shaping of other talents that could result in success off the playing field. As one former athlete stated:

I mean, I was depressed, it was like the darkest time in my life. My esteem was at its lowest point in my life. For the first time I felt helpless I guess, I couldn't just go to the gym and practice harder, go run some extra sprints, shoot some jump shots to get better, to get back in the game … I was irresponsible, I had my first child out of marriage, drinking, ya know … after I stopped playing I went through ya know, depression, what am I gonna be, what am I gonna do, I don't want to do that. Watching people that I played with for years play on TV on the next level and ya know kinda dealing with that … after I stopped playing it was sort of a stigma of people asking me like "you didn't want to go pro?" [laughing] "Nope sure didn't, wanted to work for 24,000 dollars a year, no didn't wanna play." … I mean being 6 foot 6 and black, everyone asks me "why didn't you play pro ball?" So I went through a period where I was fighting it and it was kinda like an actor named Ricky when he was a child and now he wants to be called Rick when he's older. I really think this whole thing is harder on brothers [Black men].

(Beamon and Bell 2011: 37)

Although he went through a range of emotions and difficulties, this athlete finally began to let his experience as a student-athlete work to his advantage. He continues to work through the depression he feels when he sees college teammates and guys from his neighborhood who are successful professional athletes. Edwards (2000) contends that over 60 percent of Black athletes who do play professionally will leave the sport financially destitute or in debt and will not have the necessary skills to make their way in the immensely competitive, high-tech workplace of today. Certainly, the overemphasis on professional sports careers, together with racism, exploitation, and intensive socialization into athletics and the **athletic identity** have consequences for the sports retirement of Black athletes. The most serious and common problem is athletes' failure to prepare for life after athletics.

Very few athletes advance through the ranks to become professionals. Most student athletes' last game is in fact the last game of their senior high school year. For college athletes, there is a less than a 1 percent chance that they will play professional sports, with the average career lasting only three and a half years (Coakley 2010). Many have a difficult time leaving behind their expectations for professional sports careers and the athletic identity they have developed. The transition from competitive athlete to non-athlete is an inevitable reality for all athletes. Whether it occurs after high school (which is most likely), college, or a professional sports career, retirement from competitive sports ensues at a relatively young age compared to other occupations. Many athletes are ill-prepared to handle life after sports and experience significant personal disruption upon retirement (Beamon and Bell 2011; Wooten 1994). The transition out of sports is especially troubling for Black student-athletes participating in revenue-generating sports. Since Black male student-athletes possess a stronger expectation to play professional sports, they are often less prepared to enter the workforce than their White counterparts (Beamon and Bell 2002; Edwards 2000; Eitle and Eitle 2002; Harrison and Lawrence 2003; Hoberman 2000; Pascarella et al. 1999). This lack of preparation for non-athletic careers manifests itself in many ways. Overall, Black athletes demonstrate lower levels of life satisfaction after retirement than other population groups (Perna, Ajlgren, and Zaichkowsky 1999).

Retirement is most often involuntary and results from **deselection**, injury, or age (Meeker, Stankovich, and Kays 2000). This process may be difficult for an athlete who has invested much of his time in college preparing and training, only to be subsequently deemed "not good enough" to advance to the next level. Athletes are exiting a highly structured, all-encompassing lifestyle that has influenced almost every aspect of their lives for many years. Meeker, Stankovich, and Kays (2000) summarized several factors contributing to the difficulty of adjusting to life without sports, including: (1) the enormous time commitment devoted to sports; (2) limited work experience; (3) demanding travel schedule; (4) diet and exercise requirements, and (5) social responsibilities.

Identity

One of the most significant difficulties for retiring athletes is redefining their identity and self-concept. Athletes participating in high-level sports competitions have often developed an exclusively *athletic* identity, with most of their self-definition and self-worth based on sport participation and success. The role of athlete takes precedence over all other roles and identities from a very early age, and this continues as long as the athlete is involved in sports. Athletic identity has been attributed to the time that is spent on and around athletics, as well as to the enormous amount of praise and social support athletes receive for success on the playing field.

As previously discussed, Blacks are especially vulnerable to the exclusivity of an athletic identity. Many Black males nurture the development of one identity, the athletic identity. Consequently, Black and Hispanic males in football and basketball have been found to have the highest rates of **identity foreclosure**, or the forced abandonment of identity later in life (Scales 1991). Black males are socialized intensely into sports by family, media, and community; consequently they are more likely to have a foreclosed athletic identity.

Athletic identity foreclosure begins in early childhood. Self-identities and social identities are composed almost exclusively of "athlete," which makes their transitions out of sports difficult when they are forced to redefine both self and social identities. Although the difficulties vary in severity and form, many athletes have trouble during the process. They held expectations that they would play professional sports and were not prepared during college to make alternate career choices after sports. Many describe feeling depressed and report feeling a loss similar to death, losing a body part, or losing a family member. They grieve and mourn for the loss of a part of themselves that has been central to their identity throughout most of their lives. Many do not know who they are without sports, how others will relate to them as a non-athlete, and/or experience a loss of status associated with being an athlete. For example, one former Division I basketball player stated that "I really didn't know how to be a regular dude, how to not be a basketball player, what that means even" (Beamon 2012). They use terms like "regular" and "normal" to describe the person they thought they should be after sports.

Even former elite athletes may be hindered by their once-glorified status as they redefine themselves as "normal." As they struggle to find a new occupation and identity, society often continues to relate to them as athletes. One athlete's comment illustrates how the loss of status can further add to the depression that many athletes feel as they retire from competitive athletics and try to redefine their identity:

It's like I said football and playing at each level, pretty much everything's done for you. I mean you used to people waiting on you hand and foot, you used to being the big man around campus, and whatever you did you're pretty much god ... Losin' that status, that was the most depressing thing to me.

(Beamon 2012: 204)

While athletic identity foreclosure is not a problem that only Black athletes face, the current literature confirms quantitatively that Black athletes are more likely than Whites to see sports as the focal point of their lives and perceive that others view them only as "athletes" (Harrison et al. 2011; Murphy, Petitpas, and Brewer 1996; Scales 1991). Race seems to affect athletic identity foreclosure similar to the manner in which it has been found to play a role in other areas such as career maturity, sports socialization, sports career aspirations, and student-athlete academic success. Blacks have a more difficult experience than Whites in all of those areas, thus compounding the problems associated with the retirement process for members of that group (Beamon 2012; Edwards 2000; Scales 1991).

Rebuilding a New Life after Sports

One of the most challenging adjustments for retiring athletes is formulating a new career path. Although many college graduates face difficulties finding a job after graduation, student-athletes tend to especially struggle in this area. While most student-athletes earn degrees, they are more likely to be ill-prepared for transitioning into non-sports occupations than students who are not athletes (Beamon and Bell 2011). Additionally, Black student-athletes are less likely than their White counterparts to graduate. Table 5.1 shows Black and White male NCAA athletes' graduation rates.

Due to schedule constraints and "voluntary" summer workouts and camps, most student-athletes are not able to hold summer jobs or internships. They often choose majors that complement athletic participation as opposed to post-graduate careers. Additionally, they may not develop networking skills or explore career options. Student-athletes are often ill-equipped for the retirement process due to their certainty while in college that they would become professional athletes and their subsequent lack of preparation for another career (Beamon and Bell 2012). For example, some are reluctant even to begin careers following college graduation because they want to exhaust all sports opportunities first. Many have negative experiences finding a career

Table 5.1 Black and White Male Graduation Rates for the NCAA Division I-Entering Class of 2005

	Black	*White*
All sports	49	63
Football	51	73
Basketball	43	59

Source: NCAA 2012c

after sports and are unprepared even to undertake a job hunt, never considering career options outside of sports. One student-athlete discussed not being selected to play professional sports and the difficulty he experienced in devising a career outside of sports because he "had no experience at anything. I couldn't work in college, couldn't really do no internships in college" (Beamon and Bell 2011: 35). Another stated:

> It was terrible trying to get a job … I had put more time in athletics than I did into academics. Ya know they had internships and things like that which I wasn't taking and other people was taking … I didn't put more emphasis on the learning end of it.
>
> (Beamon and Bell 2011: 36)

This may be an illustration of how the pursuit of a sports career leads a Black man to be placed on a "fantasy island lacking the skills necessary to propel himself into the flow of mainstream America" (Gaston 1986: 371). Although there are countless success stories of student-athletes who used sports to propel themselves into satisfying and fruitful careers, collegiate athletic participation for many Black males is not translating into social mobility or cultural capital at the levels that we would expect. So many continue to pursue sports well after the realistic possibilities have been exhausted—even to the detriment of their health and non-sports career development and goals.

Conclusion

The experience of Blacks upon retirement from athletics provides another opportunity to view sport and race as contested terrain. Athletic participation most certainly provides a number of advantages to youth regardless of one's color. It promotes the qualities of teamwork, fair play, dedication, and competition—all qualities that are critical to success throughout one's life and career. If each athlete upon retirement simply made the transition into the workplace and carried with them those qualities, sport could simply be viewed as opportunity. However, this chapter has shown that athletes, particularly Blacks, often form identities that are exclusively connected to their role as an athlete. As one invests more deeply in that identity, more realistic and healthy alternatives can get pushed to one side. As some Black student-athletes gradually and disproportionately adopt the "athlete" identity, others compound this problem. Research suggests that even faculty place an identity upon student-athletes that emphasizes the athlete, and that faculty perceptions of Black male and female student-athletes are less favorable than those of White student athletes (Comeaux 2010).

There are implications and opportunities for universities, athletes, and the Black community to improve this situation. Universities must begin to implement better programmatic thrusts aimed at preparing student-athletes for careers after sports. This could be done through intense mentoring, an internship requirement, and/or enhanced career development programs. Athletes must also take responsibility for their own futures, and begin to see sports as a "Plan B" instead of "Plan A." Although discrimination and blocked opportunities continue to exist for Blacks in society, as well as sports administration and coaching, Black families have a responsibility to encourage young men and women in other avenues of success beyond sports. Also, teachers and faculty have a responsibility to see the "student" identity as much as they see the "athlete" identity. By employing commonly held stereotypes about Blacks, teachers often develop lower expectations for Black student-athletes' educational performance (Comeaux 2010).

DISCUSSION QUESTIONS

1. What special or unique challenges do U.S. Black athletes face when they retire? Do you think that their dilemmas are different from those of White athletes? Explain.
2. Should sports ever be seen as a "Plan A" in terms of lifelong career goals?
3. Is it the responsibility of the university, the family, or the individual athlete to adequately prepare for careers after sports?

VI: Future Directions in Race and Sport Participation

⁓⁓×⁓⁓

Participation in athletic programs enables children and young adults to develop a wide range of skills. Moreover, it provides opportunities to develop trans-racial friendships, for entertainment, to cultivate belonging, and learn how to negotiate relationships while achieving shared goals. A staple in the U.S. economy, the sports industry generates millions of dollars in revenue in cities and states. For example, Super Bowl XLV alone was estimated to bring in between $200 and $300 million revenue to the North Dallas area (McCarthy 2011).

In terms of racism and racial hierarchies, although the U.S. athletics industry has moved beyond state-sanctioned segregation, racialized barriers to full participation remain. There are, for example, Blacks in areas of government and business at levels unmatched at any time in our nation's history. Of that we should be proud. To a degree, sports have been central to the development of anti-racist projects in the United States and have helped integrate some sports while others such as professional hockey remain predominantly White.

However, just like American society in general, work remains to be done in terms of race relations and sports. There have been great efforts to break down institutional discrimination in American society and in the sporting world. All major professional sports leagues and the NCAA are aware of the lack of minorities and women in decision-making positions and have policies in place to remedy this issue. Some progress has been made, but there remains an underrepresentation and a lack of opportunity for minority and female athletes to have professions related to sports after they are no longer on the field.

As we've highlighted throughout this book, it's not enough to simply discuss minorities as a single group that experiences the same obstacles in sport and society. Indeed, each minority group experiences unique challenges that have roots in their position in America's economic and cultural landscape. For instance, despite their cultural heritage of games, competitions, and physical activity, Native American players are rare on most current North American sports fields. Native Americans not only experience a lack of presence in sports, but also encounter negative imagery used for sports teams. This negative imagery can be seen in team names, mascots, and chants used by teams and fans. The fight to remove the stereotypical images of Native American mascots and nicknames in sports has been active for around four decades, and today involves many of the major Native American civil rights groups. Since the initiation of the debate some 40 years ago, more than 1,000 schools and colleges have abandoned their Native American mascots; however, many teams at all levels have yet to do so (Staurowsky and Baca 2004). Although slow change is not no change, significant strides remain to be made.

Similarly, Hispanics and Blacks experience their own unique challenges as well. While Hispanics disproportionately represent Major League Baseball players, Blacks disproportionately make up teams in football and basketball. There's nothing at all wrong with this fact alone. The potential problems lie in how much these groups have invested their resources and efforts to achieve what is statistically an unlikely outcome: professional status. This investment often comes with the cost of abandoning much more realistically attainable goals. And both of these groups experience unique challenges associated with identity. Hispanic players struggle to be accepted as "truly American." While the United States continues to grapple with immigration, baseball serves as a microcosmic view about attitudes and values related to what "American" means. On the other hand, Blacks are sometimes equated with an exclusively athletic identity by both themselves and society at large.

Representative Disparities

Despite the overrepresentation of certain racial and ethnic groups in certain sports, discussion should continue over a noticeable pattern of segregation. Black players are most visible in basketball and football. Hispanic players continue to show up most heavily in boxing and baseball. Hockey, golf, and tennis attract primarily White players—although the color barrier has been broken by star players such as Tiger Woods in golf and Venus Williams in tennis. Still, those athletes remain exceptions and one can't ignore a very visible absence of minorities in those sports. Segregation in sports is certainly dependent on the cultural factors we have discussed throughout this book as opposed to the stereotype of race-related physical characteristics. However, we can't ignore the equally important impact of socioeconomic status and access to sport. Golf, for instance, has less minority participation in large part because of the costs associated with playing on a regular basis. Minority groups such as Hispanics, Blacks, and Native Americans are the most economically disadvantaged in American society and therefore have much less access to golf and fewer opportunities for talent development.

Directions for Future Research

There are a number of directions that future research on race relations and athletics should take. First, it's imperative that researchers look more closely at the relationship between race and sport participation. As we've discussed at different points throughout this book, certain racial and ethnic groups disproportionately represent the majority of athletes in some sports, and in others they are severely underrepresented. Research should continue to identify the structural and socialization patterns that produce this phenomenon and critically analyze the consequences. Second, research should expand on racial and ethnic groups that are underrepresented in academic scholarship. We noted that some groups, such as Hispanics, Asians, and Native Americans, frequently go unstudied, particularly at the community level. Their experiences on any playing field need to be better understood in the larger context of sport participation and race/ethnicity. As researchers and students, we shouldn't assume that just because these groups may have very small levels of athletic participation, at least in certain sports, their experiences are unworthy of scholarly critique. In fact, we should also find out *why* these groups participate at the levels they do and the types of sport they play.

Third, scholars and students alike could glean more insight into sport and race with more research on the intersection of athletics and opportunity. We have argued, like Hartmann (2000), that sport is a contested terrain; that is, in some ways athletics can provide golden opportunities, but in other ways it can produce unrealistic expectations and a perpetuation of myths and stereotypes about racial and ethnic groups.

Bringing it all Together

As the first author sat at Rangers stadium and cheered for the home team, her kids cheered on their favorite player and they wildly chanted "CRUUUUUUZZZZZZ" along with thousands of other fans. In those moments no one is thinking "Is baseball too Hispanic?" None of the fans is concerned with immigration policies and whether Cruz shut out some "American" player for a slot on the Rangers roster. They were simply cheering on their favorite player who was getting the job done well for the home team. The home team: that is what sport creates for our society. A sense of "we-ness" that goes beyond race/ethnicity. We hope that America continues to follow the lead of athletics in this respect.

But sports are a microcosm of American society and, just as race still matters in American culture, it still matters in sports. The intersection of race and sports creates avenues for research and social commentary that go beyond the scope of the topics discussed in this book. Sports participation patterns and the segregation that we see in sports and sports administration will likely continue into the foreseeable future unless definitive steps are taken to eliminate such patterns. As we strive toward a truly color-blind society in America, sports can continue to lead the way as it has historically. Title IX opened up doors for women to participate on a much larger scale in a number of different sports. This increased access doesn't solely benefit women, but society at large. It debunks myths about women and athleticism and creates a broader appreciation for sport and its functions in society. Perhaps similar programs could be implemented with an emphasis on broadening racial and ethnic diversity across different sports, particularly at the high school level. Black women, for instance, should have just as much opportunity to participate in soccer as they do in basketball and track. Similarly, Black males should have greater access to high school sports such as baseball, which according to Keown (2011) is currently operating like a "country club" for higher-income Whites who can afford better equipment and training. Increased access to sport would ideally lead to greater diversity and further progress toward American race relations.

However, as we have illustrated throughout the course of this book, society must also work toward the development of realistic expectations. Athletes will continue to become overnight millionaires in some sports, but by far the vast majority of student-athletes won't. In fact, the vast majority won't even earn college scholarships to play sport. Therefore, it's imperative that sport be viewed only as one path to success, and arguably as one rare path to success. Athletics offers so many positive experiences and lessons to our youth and undoubtedly will continue to do so. But we must not ignore the problems that emerge as a result of sport becoming a multi-billion-dollar industry and the unique consequences for racial and ethnic groups.

DISCUSSION QUESTIONS

1. In what ways do you think professional athletics restricts the opportunities available to men and women—particularly those from working-class backgrounds?
2. What role can professional athletics play in countering the racism that continues in the post-civil rights United States?

References

Acker, Joan. 1990. "Hierarchies, jobs, bodies: A theory of gendered organizations." *Gender and Society, 4,* 139–58.

Adler, Patricia, and Peter Adler. 1991. *Backboards and blackboards: College athletes and role engulfment.* New York: Columbia University Press.

Altbach, Philip. 1991. "The racial dilemma in American higher education." Pp 3–17 in *The racial crisis in American higher education*, ed. William Smith, Philip Altbach, and Kofi Lomotey. Albany, NY: State University of New York Press.

American Indian Movement. n.d. "National coalition on racism in sports and media." Accessed online at http://www.aimovement.org/ncrsm/index.html

American Psychological Association. 2001. "An emergency action of the board of directors: Resolution against racism and in support of the goals of the 2001 United Nations world conference against racism, racial discrimination, xenophobia, and related intolerance." Accessed online at http://www.apa.org/pi/racismresolution.html

Aschburner, Steve. 2011. "NBA's 'average' salary—$5.15M—a trendy, touchy subject." NBA.com. Retrieved August 19, 2011 (http://www.nba.com/2011/news/features/steve_aschburner/08/19/average-salary/index.html)

Azzarito, Laura, and Louis Harrison. 2008. "'White men can't jump': Race, gender and natural athleticism." *International Review for the Sociology of Sport, 43,* 347–64.

Bachman, Jerald, John Wallace, Patrick O'Malley, Lloyd Johnston, Candace Kurth, and Harold Neighbors. 1991. "Racial/Ethnic differences in smoking, drinking, and illicit drug use among American high school seniors, 1976–89." *American Journal of Public Health, 81,* 372–77.

Bailey, Richard. 2006. "Physical education and sport in schools: A review of benefits and outcomes." *Journal of School Health, 76,* 397–401.

Banks, Dennis, and Richard Erdoes. 2004. *Ojibwa warrior: Dennis Banks and the rise of the American Indian Movement.* Norman, OK: University of Oklahoma Press.

Beamon, Krystal. 2008. "Used goods: African-American student-athletes' perception of exploitation by Division I universities." *The Journal of Negro Education, 77,* 352–64.

——— 2010. "Are sports overemphasized among African-American males?: A qualitative analysis of former collegiate athletes' perception of sports socialization." *The Journal of Black Studies, 41,* 281–300.

———— 2012. "I'm a Baller: Athletic identity foreclosure among African-American former student-athletes." *Journal of African American Studies, 16*, 195–208.

———— n.d. "African-American student-athletes' perception of racism and stereotyping on campus." Forthcoming in *The Journal of Negro Education*.

Beamon, Krystal, and Patricia Bell. 2002. "Going pro: The differential effects of high aspirations for a professional sports career on African-American student-athletes and White student-athletes." *Race and Society, 5*, 179–91.

———— 2006. "Academics versus athletics: An examination of the effects of background and socialization on African-American male student-athletes." *The Social Science Journal, 43*, 393–403.

———— 2011. "Another dream deferred: The transition out of sports and into the occupational sector for African-American male former collegiate athletes." *Journal for Sport and Student-Athletes in Education, 5*, 29–44.

Beamon, Krystal, and Chris Messer. Forthcoming. "Professional sports experiences as contested racial terrain." *Journal of African-American Studies*.

Berkhofer, Robert. 1978. *White man's Indian: Images of American Indians from Columbus to the present*. New York: Random House.

Block, Melissa. 2013. "Two sisters bring Native American pride to women's NCAA." *NPR*. Retrieved April 8, 2013 (http://www.npr.org/2013/04/08/176597459/two-sisters-bring-native-america-bride-to-womens-ncaa)

Bourdieu, Pierre. 1984. *Distinction: A social critique of the judgment of taste*. London: Routledge and Kegan Paul.

Braddock, Jomills. 1991. "Bouncing back: Sports and academic resilience among African-American males." *Education and Urban Society, 24*, 113–31.

Broh, Beckett. 2002. "Linking extracurricular programming to academic achievement: Who benefits and why?" *Sociology of Education, 75*, 69–95.

Buffington, Daniel, and Todd Fraley. 2011. "Racetalk and sport: The color consciousness of contemporary discourse on basketball." *Sociological Inquiry, 81*, 333–52.

Burgos, Adrian. 2007. *Playing America's game: Baseball, Latinos, and the color line*. Los Angeles, CA: University of California Press.

———— 2009. "Left out: Afro-Latinos, Black baseball, and the revision of baseball's racial history." *Social Text, 98*, 37–58.

Callais, Todd. 2010. "Controversial mascots: Authority and racial hegemony in the maintenance of deviant symbols." *Sociological Focus, 43*, 61–81.

Carmicheal, Stokely, and Charles Hamilton. 1967. *Black Power: The Politics of Liberation in America*. New York: Vintage Books.

Carrington, Ben. 2010. *Race, sport, and politics: The sporting Black diaspora*. Los Angeles, CA: Sage.

Center for Native American Youth. 2012. "Fast facts on Native American youth and Indian Country." Accessed online at http://www.aspeninstitute.org/sites/default/files/content/upload/1302012%20Fast%20Facts.pdf

Children Now. 1999. "A different world: Native American children's perceptions of race and class in the media." Accessed online at http://www.childrennow.org/uploads/documents/different_world_native_americans_1999.pdf

Churchill, Ward. 2004. *Kill the Indian, save the man: The genocidal impact of American Indian residential schools*. San Francisco, CA: City Lights Books.

Coakley, Jay. 2010. *Sports in society: Issues and controversies*. New York: McGraw-Hill.

Coffey, Laura. 2010. "10 ways to get a grip on sports for kids." *NBC* (July 30). Retrieved from http://www.today.com/id/32063374/ns/today-today_technology_and_money/

Comeaux, Eddie. 2010. "Racial differences in faculty perceptions of collegiate student-athletes' academic and post-undergraduate achievements." *Sociology of Sport Journal, 27*, 390–412.

Connell, Raewyn. 2005. *Masculinities* (2nd edn.). Crows Nest, Australia: Allen and Unwin.

Donnor, Jamel. 2005. "Toward an interest-convergence in the education of African-American football student-athletes in major college sports." *Race, Ethnicity, and Education, 8*, 45–67.

Dorish, Joe. 2011a. "WNBA teams with best overall attendance records." *Yahoo! Sports*. Retrieved June 6, 2011 (http://sports.yahoo.com/wnba/news?slug=ycn-8596889)

——— 2011b. "How much money do WNBA players make in salary?" *Yahoo! Sports*. Retrieved June 9, 2011 (http://sports.yahoo.com/wnba/news?slug=ycn-8612605)

Du Bois, W. E. B. 1903. *The souls of black folk*. New York: New American Library.

Edwards, Harry. 1988. "The single-minded pursuit of sports fame and fortune is approaching an institutionalized triple tragedy in Black society." *Ebony, 43*, 138–40.

——— 2000. "Crisis of Black athletes on the eve of the 21st century." *Society, 37*, 9–13.

——— 2010. "Social change and popular culture: Seminal developments at the interface of race, sport and society." *Sport in Society, 13*, 59–71.

Eitle, Tamela, and David Eitle. 2002. "Race, cultural capital, and the educational effects of participation in sports." *Sociology of Education, 75*, 123–46.

Eitzen, D. Stanley. 2000. "Racism in big-time college sport: Prospects for the year 2020 and proposal for change." Pp. 293–306 in *Racism in college athletics: The African American athlete's experience*, ed. D. Brooks and R. Althouse. Morgantown, WV: Fitness Information Technology, Inc.

——— 2003. "Sports and fairy tales: Upward mobility through sport." Pp. 405–10 in *Down to earth sociology: Introductory readings* (12th edn.), ed. J. Henslin. New York: Free Press.

——— 2012. *Fair and foul: Beyond the myths and paradoxes of sport*. Lanham, MD: Rowan and Littlefield.

ESPN. 2011. "Targeting the Hispanic baseball fan." Accessed online at http://beisbol.net/wp-content/uploads/2009/04/targeting-the-hispanic-baseball-fan.pdf

——— 2013. "NBA attendance report—2012." Accessed online at http://espn.go.com/nba/attendance/_/year/2012

Ewing, Martha, Lori Gano-Overway, Crystal Branta, and Vern Seefeldt. 2002. "The role of sports in youth development." Pp. 31–47 in *Paradoxes of Youth and Sport*, ed. Michael Margaret Gatz, Michael Messner, and Sandra Ball-Rokeach. Albany, NY: State University of New York Press.

Farry, Tom. 2008. *Game on: The All-American race to make champions of our children*. New York: ESPN Books.

Feagin, Joe, and Melvin Sikes. 1995. "How Black students cope with racism on White campuses." *The Journal of Blacks in Higher Education, 8*, 91–97.

Franks, Ray. 1982. *What's in a nickname? Exploring the jungle of college athletic mascots*. Amarillo, TX: Ray Franks Publishing.

Gallagher, Charles (ed.). 2012. *Rethinking the color line.* New York: McGraw Hill.

Gaston, J. C. 1986. "The destruction of the young Black male: Impact of popular culture and organized sports." *Journal of Black Studies, 16,* 369–84.

Gee, Sarah. 2009. "Mediating sport, myth, and masculinity: The national hockey league's 'inside the warrior' advertising campaign." *Sociology of Sport Journal, 26,* 578–98.

Gems, Gerald. 1998. "The construction, negotiation, and transformation of racial identity in American football: A study of Native and African Americans." *American Indian Culture and Research Journal, 22,* 131–50.

Graham, Renee. 1993. "Symbol or stereotype: One consumer's tradition is another's racial slur." *The Boston Globe* (January 6): 35.

Gramsci, Antonio. 1971. *Selections from the prison notebooks.* New York: International Publishers.

Gray, Amy, and Chery Smith. 2003. "Fitness, dietary intake, and body mass index in urban Native American youth." *Journal of American Dietetic Association, 103,* 1187–91.

Haggard, Dixie. 2004. "Nationalism." Pp. 224–26 in *Native Americans in sports,* ed. Richard King. Armonk, NY: Sharpe Reference.

Hall, Ronald. 2001. "The ball curve: Calculated racism and the stereotype of African-American men." *Journal of Black Studies, 32,* 104–19.

Hancock, John Lee (dir.). 2009. *The Blind Side* (film). Warner Brothers.

Harkins, Bob. 2012. "Is baseball turning into Latin America's game?" *NBC Sports.* Retrieved February 21, 2012 (http://nbcsports.msnbc.com/id/43665383/ns/sports-baseball)

Harris, Othello. 1994. "Race, sport, and social support." *Sociology of Sport Journal, 11,* 40–50.

Harrison, C. Keith. (2000). Black athletes at the millennium. *Society, March/April,* 35–39.

Harrison, C. Keith, and Suzanne Lawrence. 2003. "African-American student-athletes' perception of career transition in sport: A qualitative and visual elicitation." *Race, Ethnicity and Education, 6,* 373–94.

Harrison, Louis, Gary Sailes, Willy Rotich, and Albert Bimper. 2011. "Living the dream or awakening from the nightmare: Race and athletic identity." *Race, Ethnicity, and Education, 14,* 91–103.

Hartmann, Douglas. 2000. "Rethinking the relationship between sport and race in American culture: Golden ghettos and contested terrain." *Sociology of Sport Journal, 17,* 229–53.

Hawkins, Billy. 1999. "Black student athletes at predominantly White National Collegiate Athletic Association Division I institutions and the pattern of oscillating migrant laborers." *Western Journal of Black Studies, 23,* 1–9.

Hill, Grant. 1993. "Youth sport participation of professional baseball players." *Sociology of Sport Journal, 10,* 107–14.

Hoberman, John. 1997. *Darwin's athletes: How sport has damaged Black America and preserved the myth of race.* Boston, MA: Houghton Mifflin.

———— 2000."The price of 'Black dominance.'" *Society, 37,* 49–56.

Hylton, Kevin. 2010. "How a turn to critical race theory can contribute to our understanding of 'race,' racism and anti-racism in sport." *International Review for the Sociology of Sport, 45,* 335–54.

Iber, Jorge, Samuel Regalado, Jose Alamillo, and Arnoldo De Leon. 2011. *Latinos in U.S. sport: A history of isolation, cultural identity, and acceptance.* Champaign, IL: Human Kinetics.

Jones, Ryan. 2005. *King James: Believe the hype.* New York: St. Martin's Press.

Jordan, Will. 1999. "Black high school students' participation in school-sponsored sports activities: Effects on school engagement and achievement." *The Journal of Negro Education, 68*, 54–71.

Kalambakal, Vickey. 2004. "National Indian Athletic Association." P. 223 in *Native Americans in sports*, ed. C. Richard King. Armonk, NY: Sharpe Reference.

Keown, Tim. 2011. "Is Major League Baseball too Hispanic?" *ESPN*. Retrieved October 4, 2011 (http://espn.go.com/espn/commentary/story/_/id/7058357/are-there-too-many-hispanics-major-league-baseball)

King, C. Richard. 2004. *Native Americans in sports*. Armonk, NY: Sharpe Reference.

King-White, Ryan. 2010. "Danny Almonte: Discursive construction(s) of (im)migrant citizenship in neoliberal America." *Sociology of Sport Journal, 27*, 178–99.

Klein, Alan. 2000. "Latinizing Fenway Park: A cultural critique of the Boston Red Sox, their fans, and the media." *Sociology of Sport Journal, 17*, 403–22.

Lapchick, Richard. 1996. "Race and college sports: A long way to go." Pp. 5–18 in *Sport in society*, ed. Richard Lapchick. Thousand Oaks, CA: Sage.

———— 2008. *100 Pioneers: African-Americans who broke color barriers in sport*. Morgantown, WV: Fitness Info Tech.

———— 2011. "Racial and gender report card." Accessed online at http://web.bus.ucf.edu/sportbusiness/?page=1445

Ley, Bob (prod.). 1998. *Race and sports: Running in place?* (Television broadcast, April 14). Bristol, CT: ESPN.

Lipsky, John. 2004. *A history of Afro-Hispanic language: Five centuries, five continents*. Cambridge, MA: Cambridge University Press.

Litsky, Frank. 2003. "Study finds top teams failing in the classroom." *New York Times* (March 25). Accessed online at http://www.nytimes.com/2003/03/25/sports/2003-ncaa-tournament-academics-study-finds-top-teams-failing-in-the-classroom.html

Lopez, Ian. 2004. *Racism on trial: The Chicano fight for justice*. Cambridge, MA: Harvard University Press.

Luis, William. 2005. *The Afro-Hispanic Review, 24*, 5–7 (editor's note).

McCarthy, Michael. 2011. "Super Bowl XLV set to bring record revenue to Texas." *USA Today*, (February 3). Accessed online at http://usatoday30.usatoday.com/sports/football/nfl/2011-02-03-super-bowl-revenue_N.htm

McPherson, Barry, James Curtis, and John Loy. 1989. *The social significance of sport*. Champaign, IL: Human Kinetics Books.

Maloney, Michael, and Robert McCormick. 1993. "An examination of the role that intercollegiate athletic participation plays in academic achievement: Athletes' feats in the classroom." *The Journal of Human Resources, 28*, 555–70.

Marx, Karl. 1867. *Capital: Volume I: Critique of Political Economy*. New York: Penguin Classics.

Matthews, Christopher. 2010. "Can David Stern stop NBA players from going bankrupt?" *Bleacherreport*. Retrieved June 29, 2010 (http://bleacherreport.com/articles/413336-from-looseballs-to-loose-change bankruptcy-and-the-nba)

Meeker, Darin, Christopher Stankovich, and Todd Kays. 2000. *Positive transitions for student-athletes: Life skills for transitions in sport, college, and career*. Scottsdale, AZ: Holcomb Hathaway.

Meerskin, Debra. 2012. "Crazy Horse malt liquor and athletes: The tenacity of stereotypes." Pp. 304–10 in *Rethinking the color line,* ed. C. Gallagher. New York: McGraw Hill.

Meggyesy, Dave. 2000. "Athletes in big-time college sports." *Society, 37,* 24–29.

Melnick, Merrill, Donald Sabo, and Beth Vanfossen. 1992. "Educational effects of interscholastic athletic participation on African-American and Hispanic youth." *Adolescence, 27,* 295.

Miller, Patrick, and David K. Wiggins (ed.). 2004. *Sport and the color line: Black athletes and race relations in twentieth-century America.* New York: Routledge.

Mills, Billy. 2009. *Wokini: A Lakota journey to happiness and self-understanding,* New York: Hay House.

Murphy, Geraldine, Albert J. Petitpas, and Britton W. Brewer. 1996. "Identity foreclosure, athletic identity, and career maturity in intercollegiate athletes." *The Sports Psychologist, 10,* 239–46.

National Collegiate Athletic Association. 2006a. "NCAA report on federal graduation rates data Division I." Accessed online at http://web1.ncaa.org/app_data/instAggr2006/1_0.pdf

———— 2006b. "NCAA Sports Sponsorship and Participation Rates 1981–82—2000–2005." Accessed online at http://www.ncaapublications.com/p-3785-1982-06-participation-statistics-report.aspx

———— 2012a. "Probability of competing in athletics beyond high school." Accessed online at http://www.ncaa.org/wps/wcm/connect/public/Test/Issues/Recruiting/Probability+of+Going+Pro

———— 2012b. "Race and gender demographics." Accessed online at http://web1.ncaa.org/rgdSearch

———— 2012c. "Trends in graduation-success rates and federal graduation rates at NCAA Division I Institutions." Accessed online at http://www.ncaa.org/wps/wcm/connect/public/ncaa/pdfs/201 2/2012+gsr+and+fed+trends

National Federation of State High School Associations. 2011. "Sports Participation Data." Accessed online at http://www.nfhs.org/Participation/HistoricalSearch.aspx

Nuessel, Frank. 1994. "Objectionable sport team designations." *Names, 42,* 101–19.

Oher, Michael. 2011. *I beat the odds: From homelessness, to the Blindside, and Beyond.* New York: Penguin.

Ortiz, Maria. 2011. "Opening day: Latinos and baseball by the numbers." *Fox News Latino* (March 31). Accessed online at http://latino.foxnews.com/latino/sports/2011/03/31/opening-day-latinos-baseball-numbers/

Pandya, Sameer. 2012. "The Jeremy Lin discussion." *ESPN.com* (February 18). Accessed online at http://espn.go.com/espn/commentary/story/_/id/7581502/the-racial-complexion-jeremy-lin-discussion

Pascarella, Ernest, Rachael Truckenmiller, Amaury Nora, Patrick Terenzini, Marsha Edison, and Linda Hagedorn. 1999. "Cognitive impacts of intercollegiate athletic participation: Some further evidence." *The Journal of Higher Education, 70,* 1–26.

Pate, Russell, Stewart Trost, Sarah Levin, and Marsha Dowda. 2000. "Sports participation and health-related behaviors among U.S. youth." *Archives of Pediatrics and Adolescent Medicine, 154,* 904–11.

Perna, Frank, Rebecca Ajlgren, and Leonard Zaichkowsky. 1999. "The influence of career planning, race, and athletic injury on life satisfaction among recently retired collegiate male athletes." *The Sport Psychologist, 13*(2), 144–56.

Person, Dawn, Marcella Benson-Quaziena, and Ann Marie Rogers. 2001. "Female student athletes and student athletes of color." *New Direction for Student Services, 93*, 55–64.

Pewewardy, Cornel. 1999. "The deculturalization of indigenous mascots in U.S. sports culture." *The Educational Forum, 63*, 342–47.

Pickett, Moneque, Marvin Dawkins, and Jomills Braddock. 2009. "The effect of title IX on participation of Black and White females in high school sports: Evidence from national longitudinal surveys." *Journal of Race and Policy, 56*, 1581–603.

Price, Joseph, and Justin Wolfers. 2010. "Racial discrimination among NBA referees." *The Quarterly Journal of Economics, 125*(4), 1859–87.

Quinn, Kevin. 2009. *Sports and their fans: The history, economics and culture of the relationship between spectator and sport.* Jefferson, NC: McFarland.

Quinn, T. J. 2012. "Concern over MLB rule in Latin America." *ESPN.* Retrieved March 1, 2012 (http://espn.go.com/espn/otl/story/_/page/MLB-rule-change/major-league-baseball-rule-change-free-agent-pay-causes-concern-dominican-republic-venezuela)

Randolph Sugar, Bert. 2006. "Joe Louis' Greatest Fights: Louis–Schmeling." *ESPN.* Retrieved May 18, 2006 (http://sports.espn.go.com/sports/boxing/news/story?id=2449306)

Reilly, Rick. 2008. "Life of Reilly." *ESPN.* Retrieved July 22, 2008 (http://sports.espn.go.com/espn/print?id=3469271andtype=story)

Robinson, Jackie; as told to Alfred Duckett. 1995 [1972]. *I never had it made.* New York: HarperCollins.

Roscigno, Vincent. J. 1999. "The Black–White achievement gap, family–school links and the importance of place." *Sociological Inquiry, 69*, 159–86.

Rosenstein, Jay (dir.). 1997. *In whose honor?* [Film]. New Day Films.

Sack, Allen, and Ellen Staurowsky. 1998. *College athletes for hire: The evolution and legacy of the NCAA's amateur myth.* Westport, CT: Praeger.

Sailes, Gary. 1991. "The myth of Black sports supremacy." *Journal of Black Studies, 21*, 480–87.

——— 1998. "Betting against the odds: An overview of black sports participation." Pp. 23–35 in *African-Americans in sports,* ed. Gary Sailes. New Brunswick, NJ: Transaction Publishers.

Saint Onge, Jarron, and Patrick Krueger. 2011. "Education and racial–ethnic differences in types of exercise in the United States." *Journal of Health and Social Behavior, 52*, 197–211.

Salome, Kilkenny. 2005. "Lost wealth: The economic value of Black male college athletes." *Network Journal, 13*, 32.

Scales, J. 1991. "African-American student-athletes: An example of minority exploitation in collegiate athletics." Pp. 71–99 in *Counseling college student-athletes: Issues and interventions,* ed. Edward Etzel, A. P. Ferrante, and James Pinkey. Morgantown, WV: Fitness Information Technology, Inc.

Schaefer, Richard. 2011. *Racial and ethnic groups* (10th edn.). Upper Saddle River, NJ: Pearson.

Scott, Lawrence, and William Womack. 1992. *The Double V: The Civil Rights Struggle of the Tuskegee Airmen.* East Lansing, MI: Michigan State University Press.

Sellers, Robert. 2000. "African-American student-athletes: Opportunity or exploitation?" Pp. 133–54 in *Racism in college athletics: The African-American athlete's experience,* ed. D. Brooks and R. Althouse. Morgantown, WV: Fitness Information Technology, Inc.

Sellers, Robert and Gabriel Kuperminc. 1997. "Goal discrepancy in African-American male student-athletes' unrealistic expectations for careers in professional sports." *Journal of Black Psychology, 23,* 6–23.

Sigelman, Lee. 2001. "Hail to the Redskins? Public reactions to a racially insensitive team name?" Pp. 203–209 in *Contemporary issues in the sociology of sport,* ed. A. Yinnakis and M. Melnic. Champaign, IL: Human Kinetics.

Simpson, Kevin. 2009. "Sporting dreams die on the 'Rez.'" Pp. 285–91 in *Sport in Contemporary Society,* ed. D. Eitzen. Boulder, CO: Paradigm.

Smith, Earl. 2004. "The African-American student-athlete." Pp. 121–45 in *Race and sport: The struggle for equality on and off the field,* ed. Charles Ross. Jackson, MS: University of Mississippi Press.

———— 2007. *Race, sport, and the American Dream.* Durham, NC: Carolina Academic Press.

Smith, William, Walter Allen, and Lynette Danley. 2007. "Assume the position … you fit the description: Psychosocial experiences and racial battle fatigue among African-American male college students." *American Behavioral Scientist, 51,* 551–78.

Snyder, Eldon, and Elmer Spreitzer. 1978. *Social aspects of sport.* Englewood Cliffs, NJ: Prentice-Hall.

Spence, Christopher. 2000. *The skin I'm in: Racism, sports, and education.* Halifax, Nova Scotia: Fernwood Publishing.

Spencer, Stephen, Claude Steele, and Diane Quinn. 1999. "Stereotype threat and women's math performance." *Journal of Experimental Social Psychology, 35,* 4–28.

Spindel, Carol. 2002. *Dancing at halftime: Sports and the controversy over American Indian mascots.* New York: New York University Press.

Spivey, Donald. 1983. "The black athlete in big-time intercollegiate sports, 1941–1968." *Phylon, 44,* 116–25.

Stannard, David. 1992. *American holocaust: Columbus and the conquest of the New World.* New York: Oxford University Press.

Stapleton, Bruce. 2001. *Redskins: Racial slur or symbol of success?* San Jose, CA: Writers Club Press.

Staurowsky, Ellen, and Lawrence Baca. 2004. "Mascot controversy." Pp. 201–204 in *Native Americans in sports,* ed. C. Richard King. Armonk, NY: Sharpe Reference.

Steele, Claude, and Joshua Aronson. 1995. "Stereotype threat and the intellectual test performance of African Americans." *Journal of Personality and Social Psychology, 69,* 797–811.

Steele, Claude, and Paul Davies. 2003. "Stereotype threat and employment testing." *Human Performance, 16,* 311–26.

Thomas, David. 2000. *Skull wars: Kennewick man, archaeology, and the battle for Native American identity.* New York: Basic Books.

Upthegrove, Tanya, Vincent Roscigno, and Camille Charles. 1999. "Big money collegiate sports: Racial concentration, contradictory pressures, and academic performance." *Social Science Quarterly, 80,* 718–87.

U.S. Census Bureau. 2010. "2010 census briefs: The Hispanic population." Accessed online at http://www.census.gov/prod/cen2010/briefs/c2010br-04.pdf

Voice of America. 2009. "African-American soldiers in World War II helped pave way for integration of U.S. Military." Accessed online at http://www.voanews.com/content/a-13-2005-05-10-voa47-67929177/396374.html

Warde, Alan. 2006. "Cultural capital and the place of sport." *Cultural Trends, 15*, 107–22.

Washington, Robert, and David Karen. 2001. "Sport and society." *Annual Review of Sociology, 27*, 187–212.

Weinberg, Meyer. 1996. *Racism in contemporary America*. Westport, CT: Greenwood Press.

Wells, Stephen. 2008. "Bend it like Janiah." *Philadelphia Weekly*. Retrieved January 29, 2008 (http://www.philadelphiaweekly.com/view.php?id=14977)

Wheeler, Robert. 1979. *Jim Thorpe, world's greatest athlete*. Norman, OK: University of Oklahoma Press.

Williams, Dana. 2007. "Where's the honor: Attitudes toward the 'Fighting Sioux' nickname and logo." *Sociology of Sport Journal, 24*, 437–56.

Woodward, C. Vann. 1966. *The strange career of Jim Crow*. New York: Oxford University Press.

Wooten Jr., Ray. 1994. "Cutting losses for student-athletes in transition: An integrative transition model." *Journal of Employment Counseling, 31*, 2–10.

Glossary/Index

Note: Page numbers followed by 'f' refer to figures and followed by 't' refer to tables.

Boston Red Sox study 25

Bourdieu, Pierre (August 1930 – January 2002): a French sociologist and social theorist who developed investigational frameworks examining the role of social, economic, and cultural capital in social stratification. His theory, the cultural deprivation theory, examined the cultural reproduction of dominant class culture. This theory argues that the unequal distribution of cultural capital leads to social inequality, maintaining the dominance of the higher classes (Bourdieu 1984). 4

C

capitalism: Karl Marx (1818–1883), one of the founders of modern sociology, discussed in *Das Kapital* (1867) the motivating force of capitalism as the basis of social inequality, being the relationship between the means of production and the exploitation of the working class. This economic system is characterized by private or corporate ownership of the means of production and has the ultimate goal of making profits and accumulating capital within free competitive markets. 1

career maturity: ability to competently choose and plan career and educational goals 31, 34

careers
    after retirement from sports 42–43
    inadequate preparation for 34–35
    transition into 38–40

Chief Illiniwek: the mascot and symbol for the University of Illinois at Urbana-Champaign from 1926 to 2007, which was retired amid protest 16, 17

Chief Wahoo: the logo for the Cleveland Indians of Major League Baseball since 1947, which has drawn protest from Native American groups 15, 19

Children Now survey 18

civil rights movement: the collective organization by various groups (including Blacks) over a period, often said to be the 1960s, to protest against individual and institutional racism and discrimination 16

Cleveland Indians 16

color line: a term used historically to describe the legal segregation of Whites and Blacks, as well as other minority groups; today, it is used to described the continued economic, political, and social disparities that exist between Whites and other racial groups 2

contested terrain: the view that sport can be simultaneously understood as both a positive force and impediment for racial and ethnic groups. Positively, sports have created opportunities for success for racial and ethnic groups; however, sports have also served to perpetuate myths about race and ethnicity and are still characterized by forms of institutional discrimination. 7, 8, 19, 26, 37, 43, 47

cultural capital: a form of capital as defined by Pierre Bourdieu that includes assets such as education that can be converted into economic capital, social power, and social mobility 4, 43

culture: consists of the shared and learned set of norms, values, beliefs, practices, traditions, as well as tangible goods of a particular society or group 4

D

de facto segregation: segregation that happens in fact, or practice, but is not written into law 2

deselection: the process by which one is not deemed suitable to advance to the next level of athletic participation due to performance, ability, or potential for progress 40

Division I: the National Collegiate Athletic Association subdivides its athletic competition into three divisions, Division I, II, and III. Division I is the highest level of competition sanctioned by the NCAA. 6, 7t, 13, 14f, 31, 32, 42, 42t

dominant group: in the United States, European Americans, also referred to as 'White' or Caucasians, have been the racially dominant group that continues to hold the majority of the social, economic, and political power 15

Dominican Republic 21, 22, 24, 25, 26

Du Bois, W.E.B. 2

E

ethnicity: membership of a group sharing similar cultural characteristics such as nationality, language, or ancestry 1

F

Florida State Seminoles 16

football

academic performance of Black youth focusing on 30

Blacks in professional 5, 7t, 30f

expectation of playing in NFL 31

graduation rates in Division 1 32, 42, 42t

student athlete racial composition 14f

Super Bowl 45

use of Native American mascots in 14–15, 16

future directions in race and sport participation 45–48

G

genocide: intentional elimination or systematic killing of an entire group of people, who may or may not be the numerical minority such as Native Americans during the British colonial era 10, 15 girls' participation in high school sports 3, 3f

goal discrepancy: occurs when an individual holds unrealistic expectations to attain a goal that is possibly beyond his or her control. Goal discrepancy is a disjunction that occurs when one is unable to distinguish between following a dream and chasing a dream to the detriment of other worthy goals. 33

golf 4, 6, 34, 46

graduation rates 32, 42, 42t

H

hegemonic masculinity: the practice of affording men and maleness a position of dominance in society and subordinating women and femininity 4

hegemony: the ideological and cultural domination of the ruling class over other social classes; Antonio Gramsci used the concept in the early 20th century to discuss the various ways in which the ruling class exerts its cultural and economic position to maintain the status quo 4

Hispanics 21–26, 46

   and anti-immigration sentiments 8, 25–26

   participation in baseball 5, 21–22

   socialization into baseball 22–25

hockey 6, 29, 46

I

identity

   see **athletic identity**

identity foreclosure: commitment to a single role or identity before exploring other roles 41–42

imagery, Native American 15–17

inequalities, reproduction of social and racial 4–8

institutional racism: a system of deeply embedded inequality within social institutions based on race which leads to the unequal treatment of an entire category of people 2, 4, 6, 19, 24

J

James, Lebron 5

Jim Crow: a regimen of state segregation (the term is based on a minstrel character) which began in 1876 and characterized much of the United States, including all of the South and much of the North and West. It applied to residential housing, access to education, and laws regulating interracial marriage, among others 2, 21, 28

L
lacrosse 11, 13, 14f
leadership positions in sport 5, 6, 6f, 7t, 34, 45
Lin, Jeremy 1

M
Major League Baseball (MLB): the premier professional baseball league in the United States, which consists of 29 U.S. teams and one team based in Canada. First founded in 1869, the league now consists of the American League and the National League, culminating in the much celebrated World Series to determine a champion each year.
    Hispanics in 5, 22, 24, 25, 26–27
    Latino players, managers and coaches in 6f
    mascots in 16
    participation by race 5–6, 22, 22f
mascots 13, 14–15, 16–17, 46
meritocracy: a society in which advancement and rewards are assigned solely based on individual achievement or ability 3
Mills, Billy 11–12

N
National Basketball Association (NBA): founded in 1946, the NBA is the highest level of professional basketball in the United States. The league consists of 30 teams structured into two conferences, each with three divisions, and boasts the highest average per player salary of all major sports leagues in the United States. 1, 2, 5, 7t, 30, 39
National Collegiate Athletic Association (NCAA): with headquarters in Indianapolis, Indiana, the NCAA is the large governing body that organizes the athletic programs of more than 1,281 colleges and universities in North America 6, 7f, 13, 14f, 30, 30f, 42, 42t, 45
National Congress of American Indians (NCAI): founded in 1944, the NCAI is the most representative Native American and Alaskan Native organization that seeks to serve the broad interests of all Native tribes and groupings 16, 19
National Football League (NFL): the highest level of professional football (American) in the United States, consisting of 32 teams with two 16-team conferences, the American Football Conference (AFC) and the National Football Conference (NFC). Championship is determined by a playoff system resulting the AFC and NFC playing in the Super Bowl. 5, 7t, 31, 38, 39
National Indian Athletic Association (NIAA) 12
Native American Sports Council (NASC) 12

Native Americans 5, 6, 8, 10–20, 45–46
    activism around imagery 15–17
    impact of discrimination on 17–19
    in sports 11–13, 14t
    symbols as mascots 13, 14–15, 16–17, 46
Navarro, Jaime 25
Negro Leagues: prior to the integration of Major League Baseball, the Negro League was the professional baseball league composed of Blacks and some Latin Americans. The League produced stars such as Josh Gibson and Satchel Paige before it was dissolved after the 1948 season as Black players slowly integrated into the MLB. 21

O
Oher, Michael 5
O'Ree, Willie 29
overrepresentation in sports 6, 23, 24, 27, 32, 46

P
pan-Indianism: an example of pan-ethnicity in which Native Americans were forced through colonialism, genocide, and federal boarding schools to transcend tribal affiliations and linguistic differences to cultivate solidarity in the face of institutional racism 10
paradigm: a set of distinct themes, concepts, or common belief patterns 28
Perez, Eddie 25
popular culture: contemporary cultural patterns ideas, fashion, fads, and personalities that are widespread and mainstream in a given culture 15
power: may refer to personal power which is the ability to control the outcomes of one's own life; or social power, which is the authority and ability to influence many while recognizing one's will, even in the face of resistance 4
predominately White institutions (PWIs): refers to colleges and universities that are historically and consistently greatly composed of White students, professors, administrators, and alumni 36
prejudice: preconceived notions about individuals based on group membership 23

R
race: a socially constructed category that was denoted by German anthropologist Johann Blumenbach in 1779 to include five basic groups: Caucasoid, Mongoloid, Malayan, Ethiopian, and American. Contemporarily, this is a social and political category that is based both upon presumed ancestry, as well as differences in ancestry, skin color, hair, eyes, and national origins. However, race

is not a simple biological category as reflected in the "one-drop rule" used in the United States. 1

during social interaction. A social construct depends on variables of our interaction and the world around us, independent from an objective "existence" of the thing itself. xii

social imitation theory: a theory of socialization that describes social learning as vicarious; individuals learn social behavior, attitudes, and emotions by observing others perform the behavior and experiencing its consequences 24

social institutions: powerful social forces such as family, government, and religion that address the fundamental needs of society 2

social mobility: the movement of people from one category to the next within a stratification system 24, 29, 39, 43

socialization into sports 23–24

    Blacks 24, 31, 36, 41

    Hispanics socialization into baseball 22–25

softball 13, 14f

stereotype: irrational generalizations or oversimplifications about group members without taking individual differences into account 7–8, 23

    Black 8, 31, 36

    Native American 10, 15, 16, 18

stereotype threat: a social psychological theory explaining the manner in which people experience anxiety when faced with a situation in which the individual may confirm negative stereotypes about his/her group 18

student-athletes

    academic achievement 31–32

    beliefs in a professional sports career 30, 30–31

    Black 6, 30, 31, 32–36

    dilemmas for 32–36

    Native American 13

    racial composition by sport 13, 14f

    women 3

T

tennis 6, 29, 34, 46

The Blind Side 5

Thomas, David 14

Thorpe, Jim 11

Title IX: legislation passed to create more equality in access to social institutions for women; it was particularly influential in creating more sport opportunities for women in high school and college 2–4, 47

U

University of Illinois Fighting Illini 16, 17

Custom Materials
DELIVER A MORE REWARDING EDUCATIONAL EXPERIENCE.

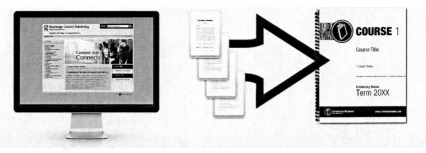

The Social Issues Collection

This unique collection features 250 readings plus 45 recently added readings for undergraduate teaching in sociology and other social science courses. The social issues collection includes selections from Joe Nevins, Sheldon Elkand-Olson, Val Jenness, Sarah Fenstermaker, Nikki Jones, France Winddance Twine, Scott McNall, Ananya Roy, Joel Best, Michael Apple, and more.

1 Go to the website at
routledge.customgateway.com

2 Choose from almost 300
readings from Routledge
& other publishers

3 Create your complete
custom anthology

COURSE 1

Course Title

Term 20XX

Learn more:
routledge.customgateway.com | 800.200.3908 x 501 | info@cognella.com